KAPLAN

Other Kaplan Books on Graduate School Admissions

Get Into Graduate School: A Strategic Approach

GRE Exam

GRE Exam with CD-ROM

GRE Biology

GRE Psychology

GRE Exam Verbal Workbook

GRE & GMAT Exams Math Workbook

KAPLAN

GRE® Exam Vocabulary Flashcards Flip-O-Matic

By the Staff of Kaplan Test Prep and Admissions

Simon & Schuster

NEW YORK · LONDON · SYDNEY · TORONTO

Kaplan Publishing
Published by Simon & Schuster
1230 Avenue of the Americas
New York, NY 10020

Contributing Editor: Justin Serrano
Project Editor: Déa E. Alessandro
Cover Design: Cheung Tai
Production Manager: Michael Shevlin
Managing Editor: Déa E. Alessandro
Executive Editor: Jennifer Farthing

September 2004
10 9 8 7 6
Manufactured in the United States of America
Published simultaneously in Canada

ISBN 0-7432-6184-4

HOW TO USE THIS BOOK

Kaplan's *GRE® Exam Vocabulary Flashcards Flip-O-Matic* is perfectly designed to help you learn 500 of the hardest, most essential GRE vocabulary words in a quick, easy, and fun way. On the front of each flashcard you'll find a GRE vocabulary word along with its part of speech and pronunciation. On the back you'll find the word's definition and synonyms, as well as a sample sentence with the vocabulary word in action. Feel free to skip over words once you've mastered them: Just clip or fold back the corner of the flashcard so that you can flip right by it on your next pass through the book. The *Flip-O-Matic* is packed with the toughest GRE vocabulary so you can flip your way to a higher score. Don't forget to flip the book over for the other half of the 500 hardest GRE words.

Good luck, and happy flipping!

ABASE

verb (uh <u>bays</u>)

a gentle breeze; something airy or unsubstantial

The *zephyr* from the ocean made the intense heat on the beach bearable for the sunbathers.

Synonyms: breath; draft

to humble; disgrace

My intention was not to *abase* the comedian.

Synonyms: demean, humiliate

ZEPHYR

noun (zeh fuhr)

the point of culmination; peak

The diva considered her appearance at the Metropolitan Opera to be the *zenith* of her career.

Synonyms: acme; pinnacle

ABATE

verb (uh <u>bayt</u>)

to reduce in amount, degree, or severity

As the hurricane's force *abated*, the winds dropped and the sea became calm.

Synonyms: ebb; lapse; let up; moderate; relent; slacken; subside; wane

ZENITH

noun (zēē nihth)

ABDICATE

verb (<u>aab</u> duh kayt)

someone passionately devoted to a cause

The religious *zealot* had no time for those who failed to share his strong beliefs.

Synonyms: enthusiast; fanatic; militant; radical

to give up a position, right, or power

With the angry mob clamoring outside the palace, the king *abdicated* his throne and fled.

Synonyms: cede; relinquish; resign; quit; yield

ZEALOT

noun (zeh luht)

ABERRANT

adj (uh <u>ber</u> unt)

passion, excitement

She brought her typical *zeal* to the project, sparking enthusiasm in the other team members.

Synonyms: ardency; fervor; fire; passion

deviating from what is normal or expected

Since he had been a steady, cheerful worker for many years, his fellow postal workers did not expect his *aberrant* burst of rage.

Synonyms: abnormal; anomalous; deviant; divergent; errant; irregular

ZEAL

adj (zeehl)

ABEYANCE

noun (uh bay uhns)

to join together

As soon as the farmer had *yoked* his oxen together, he began to plow the fields.

Synonyms: bind; harness; pair

temporary suppression or suspension

The baseball game was held in *abeyance* while it continued to rain.

Synonyms: deferral; delay; dormancy; postponement; remission

YOKE

verb (yohk)

ABJURE

verb (aab jur)

a fear or hatred of foreigners or strangers

Countries in which *xenophobia* is prevalent often have more restrictive immigration policies than countries that are more open to foreign influences.

Synonyms: bigotry; chauvinism; prejudice

to reject; abandon formally

The spy *abjured* his allegiance to the United States when he defected to Russia.

Synonyms: forswear; recall; recant; retract; take back

XENOPHOBIA

noun (zee nuh foh bee uh)

ABSCOND

verb (aab skahnd)

a ghost or specter; a ghost of a living person seen just before his or her death

Gideon thought he saw a *wraith* late one night as he sat vigil outside his great uncle's bedroom door.

Synonyms: apparition; bogeyman; phantasm; shade; spirit

to leave secretly

The patron *absconded* from the restaurant without paying his bill.

Synonyms: decamp; escape; flee

WRAITH

noun (rayth)

ABSTAIN

verb (uhb stayn)

shriveled, withered, wrinkled

The *wizened* old man was told that the plastic surgery necessary to make him look young again would cost more money than he could imagine.

Synonyms: atrophied; desiccated; gnarled; wasted

to choose not to do something

Before the medical procedure, you must *abstain* from eating.

Synonyms: forbear; refrain; withhold

WIZENED

adj (wih zuhnd)

ABSTEMIOUS

adj (aab <u>stee</u> me uhs)

charming, happily engaging

Lenore gave the doorman a *winsome* smile, and he let her pass to the front of the line.

Synonyms: attractive; delightful

moderate in appetite

Because Alyce is a vegetarian, she was only able to eat an *abstemious* meal at the Texas Steakhouse.

Synonyms: abstinent; continent; self-restraining; sober; temperate

WINSOME

adj (wihn suhm)

ABYSS

noun (uh <u>bihs</u>)

clever, deceptive

Yet again, the *wily* coyote managed to elude the ranchers who wanted to capture it.

Synonyms: crafty; cunning; tricky

an extremely deep hole

The submarine dove into the *abyss* to chart the previously unseen depths.

Synonyms: chasm; void

WILY

adj (wie lee)

ACCRETION

noun (uh <u>kree</u> shuhn)

lightly acting in a fanciful or capricious manner; unpredictable

The ballet was *whimsical*, delighting the children with its imaginative characters and unpredictable sets.

Synonyms: capricious; erratic; flippant; frivolous

a growth in size; an increase in amount

The committee's strong fund-raising efforts resulted in an *accretion* in scholarship money.

Synonyms: accumulation; buildup

WHIMSICAL

adj (wihm sih kuhl)

to fluctuate between choices

If you *waver* too long before making a decision about which testing site to attend, you may not get your first choice.

Synonyms: dither; falter; fluctuate; oscillate; vacillate

ACIDULOUS

adj (uh $\overline{\text{si}}$ juh luhs)

WAVER

verb (<u>way</u> vuhr)

sour in taste or manner

The *acidulous* taste of the spoiled milk made the young boy's lips pucker.

Synonyms: acerbic; acetose; biting; piquant; pungent; tart

undisciplined, unrestrained, reckless

> The townspeople were outraged by the *wanton* display of disrespect when they discovered the statue of the town founder covered in graffiti.

Synonyms: capricious; lewd; licentious

ACME

noun (aak me)

WANTON

adj (wahn tuhn)

highest point; summit; the highest level or degree attainable

Just when he reached the *acme* of his power, the dictator was overthrown.

Synonyms: apex; peak; summit

sickly pale

The sick child had a *wan* face, in contrast to her rosy-cheeked sister.

Synonyms: ashen; sickly

ADULTERATE

verb (uh duhl tuhr ayt)

WAN

adj (wahn)

to make impure

The restaurateur made his ketchup last longer by *adulterating* it with water.

Synonyms: debase; doctor; load

talkative, speaking easily, glib

The *voluble* man and his reserved wife proved the old saying that opposites attract.

Synonyms: loquacious; verbose

ADVOCATE

verb (aad vuh kayt)

VOLUBLE

adj (vahl yuh buhl)

to speak in favor of

The vegetarian *advocated* a diet containing no meat.

Synonyms: back; champion; support

easily aroused or changeable; lively or explosive

His *volatile* personality made it difficult to predict his reaction to anything.

Synonyms: capricious; erratic; fickle; inconsistent; inconstant; mercurial; temperamental

AERIE

noun (ayr ee) (eer ee)

VOLATILE

adj (vah luh tuhl)

a nest built high in the air; an elevated, often secluded dwelling

Perched high among the trees, the eagle's *aerie* was filled with eggs.

Synonyms: perch; stronghold

to abuse verbally, berate

Vituperating someone is never a constructive way to effect change.

Synonyms: castigate; reproach; scold

AESTHETIC

adj (ehs theh tihk)

VITUPERATE

verb (vih too puhr ayt)

concerning the appreciation of beauty

The *Aesthetic* Movement regarded the pursuit of beauty to be the only true purpose of art.

Synonyms: artistic; tasteful

thick and adhesive, like a slow-flowing fluid

Most *viscous* liquids, like oil or honey, become even thicker as they are cooled down.

Synonyms: gelatinous; glutinous; thick

AFFECTED

adj (uh fehk tihd)

VISCOUS

adj (<u>vih</u> skuhs)

phony, artificial

The *affected* hairdresser spouted French phrases, though she had never been to France.

Synonyms: insincere; pretentious; put-on

vitality and energy

> The *vim* with which she worked so early in the day explained why she was so productive.

Synonyms: force; power

AGGRANDIZE

verb (uh graan diez) (aa gruhn diez)

to increase in power, influence and reputation

The supervisor sought to *aggrandize* himself by claiming that the achievements of his staff were actually his own.

Synonyms: amplify; augment; elevate

VIM

noun (vihm)

a change or variation; ups and downs

Investors must be prepared for *vicissitudes* in the stock market.

Synonyms: inconstancy; mutability

ALACRITY

noun (uh laak crih tee)

VICISSITUDE

noun (vih <u>sih</u> sih tood)

promptness, cheerful readiness

The restaurant won a reputation for fine service since the wait staff responded to their clients' requests with *alacrity*.

Synonyms: eagerness, swiftness

to annoy, irritate; puzzle, confuse

The old man who loved his peace and quiet was *vexed* by his neighbor's loud music.

Synonyms: annoy; bother; chafe; exasperate; irk; nettle; peeve; provoke

ALLEVIATE

verb (uh lee vee ayt)

VEX

verb (vehks)

to ease, to make more bearable

Taking aspirin helps to *alleviate* a headache.

Synonyms: lessen; lighten; mitigate; relieve

trace, remnant

Vestiges of the former tenant still remained in the apartment, though he hadn't lived there for years.

Synonyms: relic; remains; sign

AMALGAMATION

noun (uh maal guh may shun)

VESTIGE

noun (veh stihj)

a merger, a uniting of elements

The *amalgamation* of the two giant companies worried the small mom and pop stores.

Synonyms: compound; fusing

related to spring; fresh

Bea basked in the balmy *vernal* breezes, happy that winter was coming to an end.

Synonyms: springlike; youthful

AMBIGUOUS

adj (aam bihg yoo uhs)

VERNAL

adj (vuhr nuhl)

doubtful or uncertain; can be interpreted several ways

The directions he gave were so *ambiguous* that we disagreed on which way to turn.

Synonyms: obscure; unclear; vague

green with vegetation; inexperienced

He wandered deep into the *verdant* woods in search of mushrooms and other edible flora.

Synonyms: grassy; leafy; wooded

AMELIORATE

verb (uh meel yuhr ayt)

VERDANT

adj (vuhr dnt)

to make better; to improve

The doctor was able to *ameliorate* the patient's suffering using painkillers.

Synonyms: pacify; upgrade; make more tolerable

wordy

The professor's answer was so *verbose* that his student forgot what the original question had been.

Synonyms: longwinded; loquacious; prolix; superfluous

AMORTIZE

verb (uh mohr tiez)

VERBOSE

adj (vuhr <u>bohs</u>)

to diminish by installment payments

While college students are notorious for accumulating credit card debt, they are not as well known for *amortizing* it.

filled with truth and accuracy

She had a reputation for *veracity*, so everyone trusted her description of events.

Synonyms: candor; exactitude; fidelity; probity

AMULET

noun (aam yoo liht)

VERACITY

noun (vuhr aa sih tee)

ornament worn as a charm against evil spirits

Though she claimed it was not because of superstition, Vivian always wore an *amulet* around her neck.

Synonyms: fetish; talisman

to respect deeply

> In a traditional Confucian society, the young *venerate* their elders, deferring to their elders' wisdom and experience.

Synonyms: adore; honor; idolize; revere

ANACHRONISM

noun (uh naak ruh nih suhm)

VENERATE

verb (vehn uhr ayt)

something out of place in time

The aging hippie used *anachronistic* phrases like 'groovy' and 'far out' that had not been popular for years.

Synonyms: archaism; incongruity

respected because of age

All of the villagers sought the *venerable* woman's advice whenever they had a problem.

Synonyms: distinguished; elderly; respectable

ANALGESIA

noun (aah nuhl jee zhuh)

VENERABLE

adj (veh nehr uh buhl)

a lessening of pain without loss of consciousness

After having her appendix removed, Tatiana welcomed the *analgesia* that the painkillers provided.

varied; marked with different colors

The *variegated* foliage of the jungle allows it to support thousands of animal species.

Synonym: diversified

ANALOGOUS

adj (uh naal uh guhs)

VARIEGATED

adj (vaar ee uh gayt ehd)

similar or alike in some way; equivalent to

His mother argued that not going to college was *analogous* to throwing his life away.

Synonyms: alike; comparable; parallel; similar

to physically sway, to be indecisive

The customer held up the line as he *vacillated* between chocolate-chip or rocky-road ice cream.

Synonyms: dither; falter; fluctuate; oscillate; waver

ANODYNE

noun (aah nuh dien)

VACILLATE

verb (vaa sihl ayt)

something that calms or soothes pain

The *anodyne* massage helped remove the knots from the lawyer's tense shoulders.

Synonyms: opiate

the practice of lending money at exorbitant rates

The moneylender was convicted of *usury* when it was discovered that he charged 50 percent interest on all his loans.

Synonym: loan-sharking

ANOMALY

noun (uh nahm uh lee)

USURY

noun (yoo zhuh ree)

deviation from what is normal

Albino animals may display too great an *anomaly* in their coloring to attract normally colored mates.

Synonyms: aberration; abnormality; deviation; irregularity

to scold sharply

The teacher *upbraided* the student for scrawling graffiti all over the walls of the school.

Synonyms: berate; chide; rebuke; reproach; tax

ANTAGONIZE

verb (aan taa guh niez)

UPBRAID

verb (uhp brayd)

to annoy or provoke to anger

The child discovered that he could *antagonize* the cat by pulling its tail.

Synonyms: clash; conflict; incite; irritate; oppose; pester; provoke; vex

absolute, certain

The jury's verdict was *unequivocal*: the organized crime boss would be locked up for life.

Synonyms: categorical; clear; explicit; express; unambiguous

ANTIPATHY

noun (aan tih puh thee)

UNEQUIVOCAL

adj (uhn ee <u>kwih</u> vih kuhl)

extreme dislike

The *antipathy* between fans of the rival soccer teams made the game even more electrifying to watch.

Synonyms: animosity; animus; antagonism; aversion; enmity

unscrupulous; shockingly unfair or unjust

After she promised me the project, the fact that she gave it to someone else is *unconscionable.*

Synonyms: dishonorable; indefensible

APATHY

noun (aa pah thee)

UNCONSCIONABLE

adj (uhn <u>kahn</u> shuhn uh buhl)

lack of interest or emotion

The *apathy* of voters is so great that fewer than half the people who are eligible to vote actually bother to do so.

Synonyms: disinterest; disregard; indifference; insensibility

offense, resentment

The businessman took *umbrage* at the security guard's accusation that he had shoplifted a packet of gum.

Synonyms: asperity; dudgeon; ire; pique; rancor

APOCRYPHAL

adj (uh pahk ruh fuhl)

UMBRAGE

noun (<u>uhm</u> brihj)

of questionable authority or authenticity

There is no hard or authoritative evidence to support the *apocryphal* tales that link the Roswell, New Mexico incident to a downed U.F.O.

Synonyms: disputed; doubtful; fictitious; fraudulent

beginner, novice

An obvious *tyro* at salsa, Millicent received no invitations to dance.

Synonyms: apprentice; fledgling; greenhorn; neophyte; tenderfoot

APOSTATE

noun (uh pahs tayt)

TYRO

noun (<u>tie</u> roh)

one who renounces a religious faith

So that he could divorce his wife, the king scoffed at the church doctrines and declared himself an *apostate*.

Synonyms: defector; deserter; traitor

swollen as from a fluid, bloated

In the process of osmosis, water passes through the walls of *turgid* cells, ensuring that they never contain too much water.

Synonym: distended

APPROBATION

noun (aa pruh bay shuhn)

TURGID

adj (tuhr jihd)

approval and praise

The *approbation* that comedian Jerry Lewis received in France included a medal from the Ministry of Culture.

Synonyms: acclaim; adulation; applause; commendation; compliments

acute, sharp, incisive; forceful, effective

Tyrone's *trenchant* observations in class made him the professor's favorite student.

Synonyms: biting; caustic; cutting; keen

ARBITRARY

adj (ahr bih trayr ee)

determined by chance or impulse

When you lack the information to judge what to do next, you are forced to make an *arbitrary* decision.

Synonyms: changeable; erratic; indiscriminate; random; wayward

TRENCHANT

adj (<u>trehn</u> chuhnt)

temporary, lasting a brief time

The reporter lived in *transitory* lodgings, staying in one place only long enough to cover the current story.

Synonyms: ephemeral; evanescent; fleeting; impermanent; momentary

ARBITRATE

verb (ahr bih trayt)

TRANSITORY

adj (<u>trahn</u> sih tohr ee)

to judge a dispute between two opposing parties

Since the couple could not come to an agreement, a judge was forced to *arbitrate* their divorce proceedings.

Synonyms: adjudge; adjudicate; determine; intermediate; intervene; judge; moderate; referee; rule

extreme mental and physical sluggishness

After surgery, the patient's *torpor* lasted several hours until the anesthesia wore off.

Synonyms: apathy; languor

ARCHAIC

adj (ahr kay ihk)

TORPOR

noun (tohr puhr)

ancient, old-fashioned

Her *archaic* Commodore computer could not run the latest software.

Synonyms: obsolete; outdated; vintage

a book (usually large and academic)

The teacher was forced to refer to various *tomes* to find the answer to the advanced student's question.

Synonyms: codex; volume

ARDOR

noun (ahr duhr)

TOME

noun (tohm)

intense and passionate feeling

Bishop's *ardor* for landscape was evident when he passionately described the beauty of the scenic Hudson Valley.

Synonyms: devotion; enthusiasm; fervency; fervidity; fervidness; fervor; fire; passion; zeal; zealousness

one who flatters in the hope of gaining favors

The king was surrounded by *toadies* who rushed to agree with whatever outrageous thing he said.

Synonyms: parasite; sycophant

ARROGATE

verb (aa ruh gayt)

TOADY

noun (<u>toh</u> dee)

to claim without justification; to claim for oneself without right

Gretchen watched in astonishment as her boss *arrogated* the credit for her brilliant work on the project.

Synonyms: appropriate; presume; take

long, harsh speech or verbal attack

Observers were shocked at the manager's *tirade* over such a minor mistake.

Synonyms: diatribe; fulmination; harangue; obloquy; revilement; vilification

ARTICULATE

adj (ahr tih kyuh luht)

TIRADE

noun (<u>tie</u> rayd)

able to speak clearly and expressively

She is extremely *articulate* when it comes to expressing her pro-labor views; as a result, unions are among her strongest supporters.

Synonyms: eloquent; expressive; fluent; lucid; silver-tongued; smooth-spoken

earthly; down-to-earth, commonplace

Many "extraterrestrial" objects turn out to be *terrestrial* in origin, as when flying saucers turn out to be normal airplanes.

Synonyms: earthbound; mundane; sublunary; tellurian; terrene

ASSAIL

verb (uh sayl)

TERRESTRIAL

adj (tuh reh stree uhl)

to attack, assault

The foreign army will try to *assail* our bases, but they will not be successful in their attack.

Synonyms: beset; strike; storm

gaudy, cheap, showy

> The performer changed into her *tawdry*, spangled costume and stepped out onto the stage to do her show.

Synonyms: flashy; loud; meretricious

ASSAGE

verb (uh swayj) (uh swayzh) (uh swahzh)

TAWDRY

adj (<u>taw</u> dree)

to make something unpleasant less severe

Like many people, Philip used food to *assuage* his sense of loneliness.

Synonyms: allay; alleviate; appease; ease; lighten; mitigate; mollify; pacify

digressing, diverting

Your argument is interesting, but it's *tangential* to the matter at hand, so I suggest we get back to the point.

Synonyms: digressive; extraneous; inconsequential; irrelevant; peripheral

ATTENUATE

verb (uh tehn yoo ayt)

TANGENTIAL

adj (taan jehn shuhl)

to reduce in force or degree; to weaken

The Bill of Rights *attenuated* the traditional power of government to change laws at will.

Synonyms: debilitate; devitalize; dilute; enervate; enfeeble; rarefy; sap; thin; undermine; undo; unnerve; water; weaken

claw of an animal, especially a bird of prey

A vulture holds its prey in its *talons* while it dismembers it with its beak.

Synonyms: claw; nail

AUDACIOUS

adj (aw day shuhs)

TALON

noun (taa luhn)

fearless and daring

The *audacious* peasant dared to insult the king's mother.

Synonyms: adventuresome; assertive; bold; brave; courageous; daring

silent, not talkative

The clerk's *taciturn* nature earned him the nickname Silent Bob.

Synonyms: laconic; reticent

AUGURY

noun (aw gyuh ree) (aw guh ree)

TACITURN

adj (<u>taa</u> sih tuhrn)

prophecy; prediction of events

Troy hoped the rainbow was an *augury* of good things to come.

Synonyms: auspices; harbinger; omen; portent; presage

done without using words

Although not a word was said, everyone in the room knew that a *tacit* agreement had been made about what course of action to take.

Synonyms: implicit; implied; undeclared; unsaid; unuttered

AUGUST

adj (aw guhst)

TACIT

adj (taa siht)

dignified, grandiose

The *august* view of the Grand Teton summit took my breath away.

Synonyms: admirable; awesome; grand; majestic

temporary irregularity in musical rhythm

A jazz enthusiast will appreciate the use of *syncopation* in this musical genre.

AUSTERE

adj (aw steer)

SYNCOPATION

noun (sihn cuh <u>pay</u> shun)

severe or stern in appearance; undecorated

The lack of decoration makes Zen temples seem *austere* to the untrained eye.

Synonyms: bleak; dour; grim; hard; harsh; severe

cooperation, mutual helpfulness

> The rhino and the tick-eating bird live in *symbiosis*; the rhino gives the bird food in the form of ticks, and the bird rids the rhino of parasites.

Synonyms: association; interdependence

KAPLAN

AXIOM

noun (aak see uhm)

SYMBIOSIS

noun (sihm bee <u>oh</u> sihs)

premise; postulate; self-evident truth

Halle lived her life based on the *axioms* her grandmother had passed on to her.

Synonyms: adage; apothegm; aphorism; maxim; rule

a self-serving flatterer, yes-man

Dreading criticism, the actor surrounded himself with admirers and *sycophants*.

Synonyms: bootlicker; fawner; lickspittle; toady

BANAL

adj (buh naal) (bay nuhl) (buh nahl)

SYCOPHANT

noun (<u>sih</u> kuh fuhnt)

predictable; clichéd, boring

His conversation consisted of *banal* phrases like 'Have a nice day' or 'Another day, another dollar.'

Synonyms: bland; clichéd; commonplace; tired; trite; vapid; worn-out

a person devoted to pleasure and luxury

A confirmed *sybarite*, the nobleman fainted at the thought of having to leave his palace and live in a small cottage.

Synonyms: hedonist; pleasuremonger; sensualist

BELFRY

noun (behl free)

SYBARITE

noun (<u>sih</u> buh riet)

bell tower; room in which a bell is hung

The town was shocked when a bag of money was found stashed in the old *belfry* of the church.

Synonyms: spire; steeple

rude and bad-tempered

When asked to clean the windshield, the *surly* gas station attendant tossed a dirty rag at the customer and walked away.

Synonyms: gruff; grumpy; testy

BEVY

noun (beh vee)

SURLY

adj (suhr lee)

group

As predicted, a *bevy* of teenagers surrounded the rock star's limousine.

Synonyms: band; bunch; gang; pack; troop

excessive amount

Because of the *surfeit* of pigs, pork prices have never been lower.

Synonyms: glut; plethora; repletion; superfluity; surplus

BIFURCATE

verb (bī fuhr kayt) (bi fuhr kayt)

SURFEIT

noun (<u>suhr</u> fiht)

divide into two parts

The large corporation just released a press statement announcing its plans to *bifurcate.*

Synonym: bisect

to replace (another) by force; to take the place of

The overthrow of the government meant a new leader to *supplant* the tyrannical former one.

Synonyms: displace; supersede

BILK

verb (bihlk)

to cheat, defraud

When the greedy salesman realized that his customer spoke poor French, he *bilked* the tourist out of 20 euros.

Synonyms: beat; defraud; diddle; gyp; overreach

SUPPLANT

verb (suh plaant)

to tarnish, taint

With the help of a public relations firm, he was able to restore his *sullied* reputation.

Synonyms: besmirch; defile

BLIGHT

verb (bliet)

SULLY

verb (suh lee)

to afflict; to destroy

The farmers feared that the night's frost would *blight* the potato crops entirely.

Synonyms: damage; plague

lofty or grand

The music was so *sublime* that it transformed the rude surroundings into a special place.

Synonyms: august; exalted; glorious; grand; magnificent; majestic; noble; resplendent; superb

BLITHE

adj (blieth)

SUBLIME

adj (suh <u>bliem</u>)

joyful, cheerful, or without appropriate thought

Summer finally came, and the *blithe* students spent their days at the beach.

Synonyms: carefree; lighthearted; merry

trick designed to deceive an enemy

> The Trojan Horse must be one of the most successful military *stratagems* used throughout history.

Synonyms: artifice; feint; maneuver; ruse; while

BOLSTER

verb (bohl stuhr)

STRATAGEM

noun (straa tuh juhm)

to support; to prop up

The presence of giant footprints *bolstered* the argument that Bigfoot was in the area.

Synonyms: brace; buttress; crutch; prop; stay; support; sustain; underpinning; uphold

unemotional, lacking sensitivity

The prisoner appeared *stolid* and unaffected by the judge's harsh sentence.

Synonyms: apathetic; impassive; indifferent; phlegmatic; stoical; unconcerned

BOMBASTIC

adj (bahm baast ihk)

STOLID

adj (stah lihd)

pompous in speech and manner

Mussolini's speeches were mostly *bombastic*; his boasting and outrageous claims had no basis in fact.

Synonyms: bloated; declamatory; fustian; grandiloquent; grandiose; high-flown; magniloquent; orotund; pretentious; rhetorical; self-important

a mark of shame or discredit

In *The Scarlet Letter* Hester Prynne was required to wear the letter 'A' on her clothes as a public *stigma* for her adultery.

Synonyms: blemish; blot; opprobrium; stain; taint

KAPLAN

BONHOMIE

noun (bah nuh mee)

STIGMA

noun (<u>stihg</u> mah)

good-natured geniality; atmosphere of good cheer

The aspects of her job that Dana loved the most were the flexible hours and the pleasant *bonhomie* in the office.

extremely loud

Cullen couldn't hear her speaking over the *stentorian* din of the game on TV.

Synonyms: clamorous; noisy

BOOR

noun (bohr)

STENTORIAN

adj (stehn tohr ee yehn)

crude person, one lacking manners or taste

“That utter *boor* ruined my recital with his constant guffawing!” wailed the pianist.

Synonyms: clod; lout; oaf; vulgarian; yahoo

a state of static balance or equilibrium; stagnation

The rusty, ivy-covered World War II tank had obviously been in *stasis* for years.

Synonyms: inertia; standstill

BURGEON

verb (buhr juhn)

STASIS

noun (stay sihs)

to grow and flourish

Faulkner neither confirmed nor denied stories about himself, allowing rumor to *burgeon* where it would.

Synonyms: bloom; burgeon; flourish; prosper; thrive

frolicsome, playful

The lakeside vacation meant more *sportive* opportunities for the kids than the wine tour through France.

Synonyms: frisky; merry

BURNISH

verb (buhr nihsh)

SPORTIVE

adj (spohr tihv)

to polish

He *burnished* the silver coffee pot until it shone brightly.

Synonyms: buff; luster; polish; scour

deceptively attractive; seemingly plausible but fallacious

> The student's *specious* excuse for being late sounded legitimate, but was proved otherwise when his teacher called his home.

Synonyms: illusory; ostensible; plausible; sophistic; spurious

KAPLAN

CABAL

noun (kuh bahl)

SPECIOUS

adj (spee shuhs)

a secret group seeking to overturn something

The boys on the street formed a *cabal* to keep girls out of their tree house.

Synonyms: camp; circle; clan; clique; coterie; in-group; mafia; mob; ring

highly self-disciplined; frugal, austere

When he was in training, the athlete preferred to live in a *spartan* room so he could shut out all distractions.

Synonyms: restrained; simple

CACOPHONY

noun (kuh kah fuh nee)

SPARTAN

adj (spahr tihn)

harsh, jarring noise

The junior high orchestra created an almost unbearable *cacophony* as they tried to tune their instruments.

Synonyms: chaos; clamor; din; discord; disharmony; noise

causing sleep or lethargy

The movie proved to be so *soporific* that soon loud snores were heard throughout the cinema.

Synonyms: hypnotic; narcotic; slumberous; somnolent

CALUMNY

noun (kaa luhm nee)

SOPORIFIC

adj (sahp uhr <u>ihf</u> ihk)

a false and malicious accusation; misrepresentation

The unscrupulous politician used *calumny* to bring down his opponent in the senatorial race.

Synonyms: defamation; libel; slander

grammatical mistake; blunder in speech

"I ain't going with you," she said, obviously unaware of her *solecism*.

Synonyms: blooper; faux pas; vulgarism

CANARD

noun (kuh nard)

a lie

That tabloid's feature story about a goat giving birth to a human child was clearly a *canard*.

Synonyms: falsehood; falsity; fib; misrepresentation; prevarication; tale; untruth

SOLECISM

noun (<u>sah</u> lih sishz uhm)

nickname

One of Ronald Reagan's *sobriquets* was "The Gipper."

Synonyms: alias; pseudonym

CANDID

adj (kaan did)

SOBRIQUET

noun (<u>soh</u> brih keht)

impartial and honest in speech

The observations of a child can be charming since they are *candid* and unpretentious.

Synonyms: direct; forthright; frank; honest; open; sincere; straight; straightforward; undisguised

to calm down or moderate

In order to *slake* his curiosity, Bryan finally took a tour backstage at the theater.

Synonyms: moderate; quench; satisfy

CAPRICIOUS

adj (kuh pree shuhs) (kuh prih shuhs)

changing one's mind quickly and often

Queen Elizabeth I was quite *capricious*; her courtiers could never be sure which one would catch her fancy.

Synonyms: arbitrary; chance; changeable; erratic; fickle; inconstant; mercurial; random; whimsical; willful

SLAKE

verb (slayk)

a well-paying job or office that requires little or no work

The corrupt mayor made sure to set up all his relatives in *sinecures* within the administration.

CARTOGRAPHY

noun (kahr tahg ruh fee)

SINECURE

noun (<u>sien</u> ih kyoor)

science or art of making maps

Gail's interest in *cartography* may stem from the extensive traveling she did as a child.

Synonyms: charting; surveying; topography

angelic, sweet

Selena's *seraphic* appearance belied her nasty, bitter personality.

Synonyms: cherubic; heavenly

CASTIGATE

verb (kaa stih gayt)

SERAPHIC

adj (seh rah fihk)

to punish or criticize harshly

Martina *castigated* her boyfriend for not remembering her birthday.

Synonyms: admonish; chastise; chide; rebuke; reprimand; reproach; reprove; scold; tax; upbraid

aware; conscious, able to perceive

The anesthetic didn't work, and I was still *sentient* when the dentist started drilling!

Synonyms: feeling; intelligent; thinking

CATALYST

noun (kaa tuh lihst)

SENTIENT

adj (<u>sehn</u> shuhnt)

something that brings about a change in something else

The imposition of harsh taxes was the *catalyst* that finally brought on the revolution.

Synonyms: accelerator; impetus; stimulant

behavior that promotes rebellion or civil disorder against the state

Li was arrested for *sedition* after he gave a fiery speech in the main square.

Synonyms: conspiracy; insurrection

KAPLAN

CATHOLIC

adj (kaa thuh lihk) (kaa thlihk)

SEDITION

noun (sih <u>dih</u> shuhn)

---

universal; broad and comprehensive

Hot tea with honey is a *catholic* remedy for a sore throat.

Synonyms: extensive; general

trace amount

> This poison is so powerful that no more than a *scintilla* of it is needed to kill a horse.

Synonyms: atom; iota; mote; spark; speck

CAUSTIC

adj (kah stihk)

SCINTILLA

noun (sihn <u>tihl</u> uh)

biting in wit

Dorothy Parker gained her reputation for being *caustic* from her cutting, yet witty, insults.

Synonyms: acerbic; biting; mordant; trenchant

to satisfy fully or overindulge

> His desire for power was so great that nothing less than complete control of the country could *satiate* it.

Synonyms: cloy; glut; gorge; surfeit

CHAOS

noun (kay ahs)

SATIATE

verb (<u>say</u> shee ayt)

great disorder or confused situation

In most religious traditions, God created an ordered universe from *chaos*.

Synonyms: clutter; confusion; disarrangement; disarray; disorder; disorderliness; disorganization; jumble; mess; muddle; scramble; snarl; topsy-turviness; turmoil

cynical; scornfully mocking

Isabella was offended by the *sardonic* way in which her date made fun of her ideas and opinions.

Synonyms: acerbic; caustic; sarcastic; satirical; snide

CHAUVINIST

noun (shoh vuh nist)

SARDONIC

adj (sahr dah nihk)

someone prejudiced in favor of a group to which he or she belongs

The attitude that men should earn more money than women is common among male *chauvinists*.

Synonyms: biased; colored; one-sided; partial; partisan; prejudicial

ruddy; cheerfully optimistic

A *sanguine* person thinks the glass is half full, whereas a depressed person thinks it's half empty.

Synonyms: confident; hopeful; positive; rosy; rubicund

CHICANERY

noun (shih kayn ree) (shi kay nuh ree)

SANGUINE

adj (<u>saan</u> gwuhn)

deception by means of craft or guile

Dishonest used-car salesmen often use *chicanery* to sell their beat-up old cars.

Synonyms: artifice; conniving; craftiness; deception; deviousness; misrepresentation

healthful

Rundown and sickly, Rita hoped that the fresh mountain air would have a *salubrious* effect on her health.

Synonyms: bracing; curative; medicinal; therapeutic; tonic

CIRCUMSPECT

adj (suhr kuhm spehkt)

SALUBRIOUS

adj (suh loo bree uhs)

cautious, aware of potential consequences

She was *circumspect* in her language and behavior when introduced to her fiancée's parents.

Synonyms: alert; cautious; heedful; mindful; prudent; solicitous; vigilant; wary

prominent, of notable significance

His most *salient* characteristic is his tendency to dominate every conversation.

Synonyms: marked; noticeable; outstanding

CLOYING

adj (kloy ing)

SALIENT

adj (say lee uhnt)

sickly sweet; excessive

When Enid and Jay first started dating, their *cloying* affection toward one another annoyed most of their friends.

Synonyms: excessive; fulsome

shrewd, wise

> Owls have a reputation for being *sagacious*, perhaps because of their big eyes, which resemble glasses.

Synonyms: astute; judicious; perspicacious; sage; wise

COALESCE

verb (koh uh lēhs)

to grow together to form a single whole

The sun and planets eventually *coalesced* out of a vast cloud of gas and dust.

Synonyms: amalgamate; blend; coalesce; condense; consolidate; fuse; unite

SAGACIOUS

adj (suh gay shuhs)

extremely sacred; beyond criticism

Many people considered Mother Teresa to be *sacrosanct* and would not tolerate any criticism of her.

Synonyms: holy; inviolable; off-limits

COFFER

noun (kah fuhr)

SACROSANCT

adj (<u>saa</u> kroh saankt)

strongbox; large chest for money

The bulletproof glass of the *coffer* is what keeps the crown jewels secure.

Synonyms: chest; exchequer; treasury; war chest

rural

The *rustic* cabin was an ideal setting for a vacation in the country.

Synonyms: bucolic; pastoral

COGENT

adj (koh juhnt)

convincing and well-reasoned

Swayed by the *cogent* argument of the defense, the jury had no choice but to acquit the defendant.

Synonyms: convincing; persuasive; solid; sound; telling; valid

RUSTIC

adj (<u>ruh</u> stihk)

very highly ornamented; relating to an 18th century artistic style of elaborate ornamentation

The ornate furniture in the house reminded Tatiana of the *rococo* style.

Synonyms: intricate; ornate

COLLUSION

noun (kuh loo zhuhn)

collaboration, complicity, conspiracy

It came to light that the police chief and the mafia had a *collusion* in running the numbers racket.

Synonyms: connivance; intrigue; machination

ROCOCO

adj (ruh <u>koh</u> koh) (roh kuh <u>koh</u>)

humorous in a vulgar way

The court jester's *ribald* brand of humor delighted the rather uncouth king.

Synonyms: coarse; gross; indelicate; lewd; obscene

CONDONE

verb (kuhn dohn)

RIBALD

adj (<u>rih</u> buhld)

to overlook, to pardon, to disregard

Some theorists believe that failing to prosecute minor crimes is the same as *condoning* an air of lawlessness.

Synonyms: exculpate; excuse; pardon; remit

effective writing or speaking

> Lincoln's talent for *rhetoric* was evident in his beautifully expressed Gettysburg Address.

Synonyms: eloquence; oratory

CONNOISSEUR

noun (kah nuh suhr)

RHETORIC

noun (<u>reh</u> tuhr ihk)

a person with expert knowledge or discriminating tastes

Dr. Crane was a *connoisseur* of fine food and wine, drinking and eating only the best.

Synonyms: authority; epicure; expert; gastronome; gourmet

silent, reserved

Physically small and verbally *reticent*, Joan Didion often went unnoticed by those she was reporting upon.

Synonyms: cool; introverted; laconic; standoffish; taciturn; undemonstrative

CONTRITE

adj (kuhn trīet)

RETICENT

adj (<u>reh</u> tih suhnt)

deeply sorrowful and repentant for a wrong

After three residents were mugged in the lobby while the watchman was away from his post, he felt very *contrite*.

Synonyms: apologetic; regretful; remorseful

impatient; uneasy, restless

The passengers became *restive* after having to wait in line for hours and began to shout complaints at the airline staff.

Synonyms: agitated; anxious; fretful

CONTUMACIOUS

adj (kahn tuh mā̄y shuhs)

RESTIVE

adj (<u>reh</u> stihv)

rebellious

The *contumacious* teenager ran away from home when her parents told her she was grounded.

Synonyms: factious; insubordinate; insurgent; mutinous; rebellious; seditious

to return or repay

Thanks for offering to lend me $1,000, but I know I'll never be able to *requite* your generosity.

Synonyms: compensate; reciprocate

CONVOLUTED

adj (kahn vuh loo tehd)

intricate and complicated

Although many people bought the professor's book, few people could follow its *convoluted* ideas and theories.

Synonyms: Byzantine; complex; elaborate; intricate; knotty; labyrinthine; perplexing; tangled

REQUITE

verb (rih <u>kwiet</u>)

to reject the validity of

The old woman's claim that she was Russian royalty was *repudiated* when DNA tests showed she was of no relation to them.

Synonyms: deny; disavow; disclaim; disown; renounce

CORROBORATE

verb (kuh rahb uhr ayt)

REPUDIATE

verb (ree pyoo dee ayt)

to support with evidence

All the DA needed was fingerprints to *corroborate* the witness's testimony.

Synonyms: authenticate; back; buttress; confirm; substantiate; validate; verify

relaxation, leisure

After working hard every day in the busy city, Mike finds his *repose* on weekends playing golf with friends.

Synonyms: calmness; tranquility

COSSET

verb (kah suht)

REPOSE

noun (rih pohz)

to pamper, to treat with great care

Marta just loves to *cosset* her first and only grandchild.

Synonyms: cater to; cuddle; dandle; fondle; love; pamper; pet; spoil

abundantly supplied, complete

The gigantic supermarket was *replete* with consumer products of every kind.

Synonyms: abounding; full

COTERIE

noun (koh tuh ree) (koh tuh ree)

REPLETE

adj (rih pleet)

an intimate group of persons with a similar purpose

Angel invited a *coterie* of fellow stamp enthusiasts to a stamp-trading party.

Synonyms: clique; set

meal or mealtime

Ravi prepared a delicious *repast* of chicken tikka and naan.

Synonyms: banquet; feast

KAPLAN

CRAVEN

adj (kray vuhn)

REPAST

noun (rih paast)

lacking courage

The *craven* lion cringed in the corner of his cage, terrified of the mouse.

Synonyms: faint-hearted; spineless; timid

response

Patrick tried desperately to think of a clever *rejoinder* to Marianna's joke, but he couldn't.

Synonyms: retort; riposte

CREDULOUS

adj (kreh juh luhs)

REJOINDER

noun (rih <u>joyn</u> duhr)

too trusting; gullible

Though many 4-year-olds believe in the Tooth Fairy, only the most *credulous* 9-year-olds also believe in her.

Synonyms: naïve; susceptible; trusting

relief from wrong or injury

Seeking *redress* for the injuries she had received in the accident, Doreen sued the driver of the truck that had hit her.

Synonyms: amends; indemnity; quittance; reparation; restitution

CRESCENDO

noun (kruh shehn doh)

REDRESS

noun (rih drehs)

steadily increasing in volume or force

The *crescendo* of tension became unbearable as Evel Knievel prepared to jump his motorcycle over the school buses.

Synonyms: acme; capstone; climax; crest; culmen; culmination; meridian; peak

to make thinner or sparser

Since the atmosphere *rarefies* as altitudes increase, the air at the top of very tall mountains is too thin to breathe.

Synonyms: attenuate; thin

CUPIDITY

noun (kyoo pih dih tee)

RAREFY

verb (rayr uh fie)

greed; strong desire

The thief stared at the shining jewels with *cupidity* in his gleaming eyes.

Synonyms: avarice; covetousness; rapacity

witty, skillful storyteller

The *raconteur* kept all the passengers entertained with his stories during the six-hour flight.

Synonyms: anecdotalist; monologist

CURMUDGEON

noun (kuhr muh juhn)

cranky person, usually old

Ernesto was a notorious *curmudgeon* who snapped at anyone who disturbed him.

RACONTEUR

noun (raa cahn <u>tuhr</u>)

occurring daily; commonplace

The sight of people singing on the street is so *quotidian* in New York that passersby rarely react to it.

Synonyms: everyday; normal; usual

DEBUTANTE

noun (dehb yoo tahnt)

QUOTIDIAN

adj (kwo tih dee uhn)

young woman making debut in high society

The *debutante* spent hours dressing for her very first ball, hoping to catch the eye of an eligible bachelor.

Synonyms: lady; maiden

overly idealistic, impractical

The practical Danuta was skeptical of her roommate's *quixotic* plans to build a roller coaster in their yard.

Synonyms: capricious; impulsive; romantic; unrealistic

DECLIVITY

noun (dih klih vih tee)

QUIXOTIC

adj (kwihk sah tihk)

downward slope

Because the village was situated on the *declivity* of a hill, it never flooded.

Synonyms: decline; descent; grade; slant; tilt

motionless

> Many animals are *quiescent* over the winter months, minimizing activity in order to conserve energy.

Synonyms: dormant; latent

KAPLAN

DECOROUS

adj (deh kuhr uhs) (deh kohr uhs)

QUIESCENT

adj (kwie eh sihnt)

proper, tasteful, socially correct

The countess trained her daughters in the finer points of *decorous* behavior, hoping they would make a good impression when she presented them at Court.

Synonyms: appropriate; courteous; polite

inclined to complain, irritable

Curtis's complaint letter received prompt attention after the company labeled him a *querulous* potential troublemaker.

Synonyms: peevish; puling; sniveling; whiny

DECORUM

noun (deh kohr uhm)

QUERULOUS

adj (kwehr yoo luhs)

appropriateness of behavior or conduct; propriety

The countess complained that the vulgar peasants lacked the *decorum* appropriate for a visit to the palace.

Synonyms: correctness; decency; etiquette; manners; mores; propriety; seemliness

cowardly, without courage

The *pusillanimous* man would not enter the yard where the miniature poodle was barking.

Synonyms: cowardly; timid

DEFACE

verb (dih fāys)

PUSILLANIMOUS

adj (pyoo suh laa nih muhs)

to mar the appearance of, to vandalize

After the wall was torn down, the students began to *deface* the statues of Communist leaders of the former Eastern bloc.

Synonyms: disfigure; impair; spoil

sharp and irritating to the senses

The smoke from the burning tires was extremely *pungent*.

Synonyms: acrid; caustic; piquant; poignant; stinging

DEFERENCE

noun (deh fuh ruhn(t)s) (def ruhn(t)s)

PUNGENT

adj (puhn juhnt)

respect, courtesy

The respectful young law clerk treated the Supreme Court justice with the utmost *deference.*

Synonyms: courtesy; homage; honor; obeisance; respect; reverence; veneration

beauty

The mortals gazed in admiration at Venus, stunned by her incredible *pulchritude*.

Synonyms: comeliness; gorgeousness; handsomeness; loveliness; prettiness

DELETERIOUS

adj (dehl ih teer ee uhs)

PULCHRITUDE

noun (puhl kruh tood)

subtly or unexpectedly harmful

If only we had known the clocks were defective before putting them on the market, it wouldn't have been quite so *deleterious* to our reputation.

Synonyms: adverse; inimical; injurious; hurtful

boxing

Pugilism has been defended as a positive outlet for aggressive impulses.

Synonyms: fighting; sparring

DEMAGOGUE

noun (deh muh gahg) (deh muh gawg)

PUGILISM

noun (pyoo juhl ih suhm)

a leader, rabble-rouser, usually appealing to emotion or prejudice

He began his career as a *demagogue*, giving fiery speeches at political rallies.

Synonyms: agitator; inciter; instigator

childish, immature, silly

Olivia's boyfriend's *puerile* antics are really annoying; sometimes he acts like a five-year-old!

Synonyms: infantile; jejune; juvenile

DEMUR

verb (dih muhr)

PUERILE

adj (pyoo ruhl)

to express doubts or objections

When scientific authorities claimed that all the planets revolved around the Earth, Galileo, with his superior understanding of the situation, was forced to *demur*.

Synonyms: dissent; expostulate; kick; protest; remonstrate

wisdom, caution or restraint

The college student exhibited *prudence* by obtaining practical experience along with her studies, which greatly strengthened her résumé.

Synonyms: astuteness; circumspection; discretion; frugality; judiciousness; providence; thrift

DERIDE

verb (dih ried)

PRUDENCE

noun (<u>proo</u> dehns)

to speak of or treat with contempt, to mock

The awkward child was often *derided* by his 'cooler' peers.

Synonyms: gibe; jeer; mock; ridicule

the quality of behaving in a proper manner, obeying rules and customs

The aristocracy maintained a high level of *propriety*, adhering to even the most minor social rules.

Synonyms: appropriateness; decency; decorum; modesty

DESICCATE

verb (deh sih kayt)

PROPRIETY

noun (pruh <u>prie</u> uh tee)

to dry out thoroughly

After a few weeks lying in the desert, the cow's carcass became completely *desiccated.*

Synonyms: dehydrate; dry; parch

to conciliate, to appease

> Because their gods were angry and vengeful, the Vikings *propitiated* them with many sacrifices.

Synonyms: appease; conciliate; mollify; pacify; placate

DESULTORY

adj (dehs uhl tohr ee) (dehz uhl tohr ee)

PROPITIATE

verb (proh pih shee ayt)

jumping from one thing to another; disconnected

Athena had a *desultory* academic record; she had changed majors 12 times in three years.

Synonyms: erratic; haphazard; indiscriminate; random

to increase in number quickly

Although he only kept two guinea pigs initially, they *proliferated* to such an extent that he soon had dozens.

Synonyms: breed; multiply; procreate; propagate; reproduce; spawn

DIAPHANOUS

adj (die aaf uh nuhs)

PROLIFERATE

verb (proh lih fuhr ayt)

allowing light to show through; delicate

These *diaphanous* curtains do nothing to block out the sunlight.

Synonyms: gauzy; sheer; tenuous; translucent; transparent

corrupt, degenerate

> Some historians claim that it was the Romans' decadent, *profligate* behavior that led to the decline of the Roman Empire.

Synonyms: dissolute; extravagant; improvident; prodigal; wasteful

DIATRIBE

noun (die uh trieb)

KAPLAN

PROFLIGATE

adj (<u>praa</u> flih guht)

an abusive, condemnatory speech

The trucker bellowed a *diatribe* at the driver who had cut him off.

Synonyms: fulmination; harangue; invective

lavish, wasteful

The *prodigal* son quickly wasted all of his inheritance on a lavish lifestyle devoted to pleasure.

Synonyms: extravagant; lavish; profligate; spendthrift; wasteful

DICTUM

noun (dihk tuhm)

PRODIGAL

adj (<u>prah</u> dih guhl)

authoritative statement

"You have time to lean, you have time to clean," was the *dictum* our boss made us live by.

Synonyms: adage; apothegm; aphorism; decree; edict

a natural inclination or predisposition

> Her childhood love of acting, singing, and adoration indicated a *proclivity* for the theater in later life.

Synonyms: bias; leaning; partiality; penchant; predilection; predisposition; prejudice; propensity

KAPLAN

DIFFIDENT

adj (dih fih dint)

PROCLIVITY

noun (proh clih vuh tee)

lacking self-confidence

Steve was *diffident* during the job interview because of his nervous nature and lack of experience in the field.

Synonyms: backward; bashful; coy; demure; modest; retiring; self-effacing; shy; timid

complete honesty and integrity

George Washington's reputation for *probity* is illustrated in the legend about his inability to lie after he chopped down the cherry tree.

Synonyms: integrity; morality; rectitude; uprightness; virtue

DILATE

verb (die layt) (die layt)

PROBITY

noun (proh bih tee)

---

to make larger, to expand

When you enter a darkened room, the pupils of your eyes *dilate* so as to let in more light.

Synonyms: amplify; develop; elaborate; enlarge; expand; expatiate

fresh and clean, uncorrupted

> Since concerted measures had been taken to prevent looting, the archeological site was still *pristine* when researchers arrived.

Synonyms: innocent; undamaged

DILATORY

adj (dihl uh tohr ee)

PRISTINE

adj (prih steen)

intended to delay, procrastinating

The congressman used *dilatory* measures to delay the passage of the bill.

Synonyms: sluggish; putting off

to lie or deviate from the truth

> Rather than admit that he had overslept again, the employee *prevaricated* and claimed that heavy traffic had prevented him from arriving at work on time.

Synonyms: equivocate; lie; perjure

DILETTANTE

noun (dih luh tahnt)

PREVARICATE

verb (prih <u>vaar</u> uh cayt)

KAPLAN

someone with an amateurish and superficial interest in a topic

Jerry's friends were such *dilettantes* they seemed to have new jobs and hobbies every week.

Synonyms: amateur; dabbler; rookie

having foresight

Jonah's decision to sell the apartment seemed to be a *prescient* one, as its value soon dropped by half.

Synonyms: augural; divinatory; mantic; oracular; premonitory

DIRGE

noun (duhrj)

PRESCIENT

adj (<u>preh</u> shuhnt)

a funeral hymn or mournful speech

Melville wrote the poem "A *Dirge* for James McPherson" for the funeral of a Union general who was killed in 1864.

Synonyms: elegy; lament

short summary of facts

Fara wrote a *précis* of her thesis on the epic poem to share with the class.

Synonym: summation

DISABUSE

verb (dih suh byuze)

PRÉCIS

noun (<u>pray</u> see) (pray <u>see</u>)

to set right, to free from error

The scientist's observations *disabused* scholars of the notion that wheat could be turned into gold.

Synonyms: correct; dismiss; undeceive

to throw violently or bring about abruptly; lacking deliberation

Bob and Edna's whirlwind courtship *precipitated* their hasty nuptials.

Synonyms: hurl; rush

KAPLAN

DISCERN

verb (dihs uhrn)

PRECIPITATE

verb (preh sih puh tayt)

to perceive, to recognize

It is easy to *discern* the difference between butter and butter-flavored topping.

Synonyms: differentiate; discriminate; distinguish

meaningless, foolish talk

Her husband's mindless *prattle* drove Heidi insane; sometimes she wished he would just shut up.

Synonyms: babble; blather; chatter; drivel; gibberish

KAPLAN

DISPARATE

adj (dih spuh ruht) (di spar uht)

PRATTLE

noun (praa tuhl)

fundamentally different; entirely unlike

Although the twins are physically identical, their personalities are *disparate*.

Synonyms: different; dissimilar; divergent; diverse; variant; various

practical, as opposed to idealistic

While idealistic gamblers think they can get rich by frequenting casinos, *pragmatic* gamblers realize that the odds are heavily stacked against them.

Synonyms: rational; realistic

DISSEMBLE

verb (dihs sehm buhl)

PRAGMATIC

adj (praag maa tihk)

to present a false appearance, to disguise one's real intentions or character

The villain could *dissemble* to the police no longer—he admitted the deed and tore up the floor to reveal the stash of stolen money.

Synonyms: camouflage; cloak; feign

a monarch or ruler with great power

Alex was much kinder before he assumed the role of *potentate*.

Synonyms: dominator; leader

DISSONANCE

noun (dihs uh nuhns)

a harsh and disagreeable combination, especially of sounds

Cognitive *dissonance* is the inner conflict produced when long-standing beliefs are contradicted by new evidence.

Synonyms: clash; contention; discord; dissension; dissent; dissidence; friction; strife; variance

POTENTATE

noun (poh tehn tayt)

to assume as real or conceded; propose as an explanation

Before proving the math formula, we needed to *posit* that *x* and *y* were real numbers.

Synonym: suggest

DISTAFF

noun (dis taf)

POSIT

verb (pah siht)

the female branch of a family

The lazy husband refused to cook dinner for his wife, joking that the duty belongs to the *distaff*'s side.

a speaker of many languages

Ling's extensive travels have helped her to become a true *polyglot*.

DISTEND

verb (dih STEHND)

POLYGLOT

noun (pah lee glaht)

to swell, inflate, bloat

Her stomach was *distended* after she gorged on the six-course meal.

Synonyms: broaden; bulge

shrewd and practical in managing or dealing with things; diplomatic

She was wise to curb her tongue and was able to explain her problem to the judge in a respectful and *politic* manner.

Synonym: tactful

KAPLAN

DITHER

verb (dihth uhr)

POLITIC

adj (pah lih tihk)

to act confusedly or without clear purpose

Ellen *dithered* around her apartment, uncertain how to tackle the family crisis.

Synonyms: falter; hesitate; vacillate; waffle; waver

controversy, argument; verbal attack

The candidate's *polemic* against his opponent was vicious and small-minded rather than convincing and well-reasoned.

Synonyms: denunciation; refutation

DIURNAL

adj (die uhr nuhl)

POLEMIC

noun (puh <u>leh</u> mihk)

KAPLAN

---

existing during the day

Diurnal creatures tend to become inactive during the night.

Synonyms: daylight; daytime

courageous, spunky

The *plucky* young nurse dove into the foxhole, determined to help the wounded soldier.

Synonyms: bold; brave; gutsy

DIVINE

verb (dih vien)

PLUCKY

adj (<u>pluh</u> kee)

to foretell or know by inspiration

The fortune-teller *divined* from the pattern of the tea leaves that her customer would marry five times.

Synonyms: auger; foresee; intuit; predict; presage

excess

> Assuming that more was better, the defendant offered the judge a *plethora* of excuses.

Synonyms: glut; overabundance; superfluity; surfeit

DOCTRINAIRE

adj (dahk truh nayr)

PLETHORA

noun (<u>pleh</u> thor uh)

rigidly devoted to theories without regard for practicality; dogmatic

The professor's manner of teaching was considered *doctrinaire* for such a liberal school.

Synonyms: dictatorial; inflexible

crude or coarse; characteristic of commoners

After five weeks of rigorous studying, the graduate settled in for a weekend of *plebeian* socializing and television watching.

Synonyms: conventional; unrefined

DOGMA

noun (dahg muh) (dawg muh)

PLEBEIAN

adj (plee bee uhn)

a firmly held opinion, especially a religious belief

Linus's central *dogma* was that children who believed in the Great Pumpkin would be rewarded.

Synonyms: creed; doctrines; teaching; tenet

able to be molded, altered, or bent

The new material was very *plastic* and could be formed into products of vastly different shape.

Synonyms: adaptable; ductile; malleable; pliant

DOGMATIC

adj (dahg maat ihk) (dawg maat ihk)

PLASTIC

adj (plaa stihk)

dictatorial in one's opinions

The dictator was *dogmatic*, claiming he, and only he, was right.

Synonyms: authoritarian; bossy; dictatorial; doctrinaire; domineering; imperious

to soothe or pacify

The burglar tried to *placate* the snarling dog by referring to it as a 'Nice Doggy' and offering it a treat.

Synonyms: appease; conciliate; mollify

DROLL

adj (drohl)

PLACATE

verb (play cayt)

amusing in a wry, subtle way

Although the play couldn't be described as hilarious, it was certainly *droll*.

Synonyms: comic; entertaining; funny; risible; witty

profound, substantial; concise, succinct, to the point

Martha's *pithy* comments during the interview must have been impressive because she got the job.

Synonyms: brief; compact; laconic; terse

DUPE

verb (doop)

PITHY

adj (pih thee)

to deceive

Bugs Bunny was able to *dupe* Elmer Fudd by dressing up as a lady rabbit.

Synonyms: beguile; betray; bluff; cozen; deceive; delude; fool; hoodwink; humbug; mislead; take in trick

calm and unemotional in temperament

> Although the bomb could go off at any moment, the *phlegmatic* demolition expert remained calm and unafraid.

Synonyms: apathetic; calm; emotionless; impassive; indifferent; passionless; unemotional

DYSPEPTIC

adj (dihs pehp tihk)

PHLEGMATIC

adj (flehg <u>maa</u> tihk)

suffering from indigestion; gloomy and irritable

The *dyspeptic* young man cast a gloom over the party the minute he walked in.

Synonyms: acerb; melancholy; morose; solemn; sour

a person who is guided by materialism and is disdainful of intellectual or artistic values

The *philistine* never even glanced at the rare violin in his collection but instead kept an eye on its value and sold it at a profit.

Synonyms: boor; bourgeois; capitalist; clown; lout; materialist; vulgarian

EBULLIENT

adj (ih byool yuhnt) (ih buhl yuhnt)

exhilarated, full of enthusiasm and high spirits

The *ebullient* child exhausted the baby-sitter, who lacked the energy to keep up with her.

Synonyms: ardent; avid; bubbly; zestful

PHILISTINE

noun (fihl uh steen)

charity; a desire or effort to promote goodness

> The Metropolitan Museum of Art owes much of its collection to the *philanthropy* of private collectors who willed their estates to the museum.

Synonyms: altruism; humanitarianism

ECLECTIC

adj (ih klehk tihk) (eh klehk tihk)

PHILANTHROPY

noun (fihl aan throh pee)

selecting from or made up from a variety of sources

Budapest's architecture is an *eclectic* mix of eastern and western styles.

Synonyms: broad; catholic; selective

a compact or close-knit body of people, animals, or things

A *phalanx* of guards stood outside the prime minister's home day and night.

Synonyms: legion; mass

EDIFY

verb (eh duh fie)

PHALANX

noun (<u>fay</u> laanks)

KAPLAN

to instruct morally and spiritually

The guru was paid to *edify* the actress in the ways of Buddhism.

Synonyms: educate; enlighten; guide; teach

to be present throughout, to permeate

Four spices—cumin, turmeric, coriander and cayenne—*pervade* almost every Indian dish, and give the cuisine its distinctive flavor.

Synonyms: imbue; infuse; penetrate; permeate; suffuse

EFFICACY

noun (eh fih kuh see)

PERVADE

verb (puhr vayd)

effectiveness

The *efficacy* of penicillin was unsurpassed when it was first introduced, completely eliminating almost all bacterial infections.

Synonyms: dynamism; effectiveness; efficiency; force; power; productiveness; proficiency; strength; vigor

shrewd, astute, keen-witted

Inspector Poirot used his *perspicacious* mind to solve mysteries.

Synonyms: insightful; intelligent; sagacious

EFFIGY

noun (eh fuh jee)

PERSPICACIOUS

adj (puhr spuh <u>kay</u> shuhs)

stuffed doll; likeness of a person

In England, *effigies* of the historic rebel Guy Fawkes are burned to celebrate his capture.

Synonyms: dummy; figure; image

to penetrate

This miraculous new cleaning fluid is able to *permeate* stains and dissolve them in minutes!

Synonyms: imbue; infuse; pervade; suffuse

EFFRONTERY

noun (ih fruhnt uhr ee) (eh fruhnt uhr ee)

PERMEATE

verb (<u>puhr</u> mee ayt)

impudent boldness; audacity

The receptionist had the *effrontery* to laugh out loud when the CEO tripped over a computer wire and fell flat on his face.

Synonyms: brashness; gall; nerve; presumption; temerity

wandering from place to place, especially on foot

Eleana's *peripatetic* meanderings took her all over the countryside in the summer months.

Synonyms: itinerant; nomadic; wayfaring

ELEGY

noun (eh luh jee)

PERIPATETIC

adj (peh ruh puh <u>teh</u> tihk)

a sorrowful poem or speech

Though Thomas Gray's *Elegy* is about death and loss, it urges its readers to endure this life, and to trust in spirituality.

Synonyms: dirge; lament

done in a routine way; indifferent

The machine-like teller processed the transaction and gave the waiting customer a *perfunctory* smile.

Synonyms: apathetic; automatic; mechanical

ELOQUENT

adj (ehl uh kwunt)

PERFUNCTORY

adj (pur <u>fuhnk</u> tuhr ee)

persuasive and moving, especially in speech

The Gettysburg Address is moving not only because of its lofty sentiments but because of its *eloquent* words.

Synonyms: articulate; expressive; fluent; meaningful; significant; smooth-spoken

willing to betray one's trust

The actress's *perfidious* companion revealed all of her intimate secrets to the gossip columnist.

Synonyms: disloyal; faithless; traitorous; treacherous

EMBELLISH

verb (ehm behl ihsh)

PERFIDIOUS

adj (puhr <u>fih</u> dee uhs)

to add ornamental or fictitious details

Britt *embellished* her résumé, hoping to make the lowly positions she had held seem more important.

Synonyms: adorn; bedeck; elaborate; embroider; enhance; exaggerate

to wander from place to place; to travel, especially on foot

Shivani enjoyed *peregrinating* the expansive grounds of Central Park.

Synonyms: journey; traverse; trek

EMULATE

verb (ehm yuh layt)

PEREGRINATE

verb (peh ruh gruh nayt)

to copy, to try to equal or excel

The graduate student sought to *emulate* his professor in every way, copying not only how she taught but also how she conducted herself outside of class.

Synonyms: ape; imitate; simulate

an oppressive lack of resources (as money); severe poverty

Once a famous actor, he eventually died in *penury* and anonymity.

Synonyms: destitution; impoverishment

ENCOMIUM

noun (ehn koh me uhm)

PENURY

noun (<u>pehn</u> yuh ree)

warm praise

Georgias's "*Encomium* to Helen" was written as a tribute to Helen of Troy.

Synonyms: citation; eulogy; panegyric; salutation; tribute

having bad connotations; disparaging

> The teacher scolded Mark for his unduly *pejorative* comments about his classmate's presentation.

Synonyms: belittling; dismissive; insulting

ENDEMIC

adj (ehn deh mihk)

PEJORATIVE

adj (peh jaw ruh tihv)

KAPLAN

belonging to a particular area; inherent

The health department determined that the outbreak was *endemic* to the small village, so it quarantined the inhabitants before the virus could spread.

Synonyms: indigenous; local; native

someone who shows off learning

The graduate instructor's tedious and excessive commentary on the subject soon gained her a reputation as a *pedant*.

Synonyms: doctrinaire; nit-picker; pedagogue; scholar; schoolmaster; sophist

ENERVATE

verb (ehn uhr vayt)

PEDANT

noun (peh daant)

to reduce in strength

The guerrillas hoped that a series of surprise attacks would *enervate* the regular army.

Synonyms: debilitate; enfeeble; sap; weaken

minor sin or offense

Gabriel tends to harp on his brother's *peccadillos* and never lets him live them down.

Synonyms: failing; fault; lapse; misstep

ENGENDER

verb (ehn jehn duhr)

PECCADILLO

noun (pehk uh dih loh)

to produce, cause, or bring about

His fear and hatred of clowns was *engendered* when he witnessed a bank robbery carried out by five men wearing clown suits and make-up.

Synonyms: beget; generate; procreate; proliferate; reproduce; spawn

causing disease

Bina's research on the origins of *pathogenic* microorganisms should help stop the spread of disease.

Synonyms: infecting; noxious

ENIGMA

noun (ih nig muh)

PATHOGENIC

adj (paa thoh <u>jehn</u> ihk)

a puzzle, a mystery

Speaking in riddles and dressed in old robes, the artist gained a reputation as something of an *enigma*.

Synonyms: conundrum; perplexity

piece of literature or music imitating other works

The singer's clever *pastiche* of the well-known children's story had the audience rolling in the aisles.

Synonyms: medley; spoof

ENUMERATE

verb (ih noo muhr ayt)

to count, list, itemize

Before making his decision, Jacob asked the waiter to *enumerate* the different varieties of ice cream that the restaurant carried.

Synonyms: catalog; index; tabulate

PASTICHE

noun (pah <u>steesh</u>)

to ward off or deflect, especially by a quick-witted answer

Kari *parried* every question the army officers fired at her, much to their frustration.

Synonyms: avoid; evade; repel

EPHEMERAL

adj (ih fehm uhr uhl)

PARRY

verb (paar ree)

lasting a short time

The lives of mayflies seem *ephemeral* to us, since the flies' average life span is a matter of hours.

Synonyms: evanescent; fleeting; momentary; transient

discussion, usually between enemies

The *parley* between the rival cheerleading teams resulted in neither side admitting that they copied the other's dance moves.

Synonyms: debate; dialogue; negotiations; talks

EPICURE

noun (eh pih kyoor) (eh pih kyuhr)

PARLEY

noun (<u>par</u> lee)

person with refined taste in food and wine

Niren is an *epicure* who always throws the most splendid dinner parties.

Synonyms: bon vivant; connoisseur; gastronome; gastronomer; gastronomist; gourmand; gourmet

an outcast

> Once he betrayed those in his community, he was banished and lived the life of a *pariah*.

Synonyms: castaway; derelict; leper; offscouring; untouchable

EQUIVOCATE

verb (ih kwihv uh kayt)

PARIAH

noun (puh rie uh)

to use expressions of double meaning in order to mislead

When faced with criticism of his policies, the politician *equivocated* and left all parties thinking he agreed with them.

Synonyms: hedge; waffle

to trim off excess, reduce

The cook's hands were sore after she *pared* hundreds of potatoes for the banquet.

Synonyms: clip; peel

ERRATIC

adj (ih raat ihk)

PARE

verb (payr)

wandering and unpredictable

The plot seemed predictable until it suddenly took a series of *erratic* turns that surprised the audience.

Synonyms: capricious; inconstant; irresolute; whimsical

model of excellence or perfection

He is the *paragon* of what a judge should be: honest, intelligent, hardworking, and just.

Synonyms: apotheosis; ideal; quintessence; standard

ERSATZ

adj (uhr sats) (uhr sats)

PARAGON

noun (<u>par</u> uh gohn)

fake, artificial

Edda, a fashion maven, knew instantly that her friend's new Kate Spade bag was really an *ersatz* version purchased on the street.

Synonyms: false; imitation

a contradiction or dilemma

It is a *paradox* that those most in need of medical attention are often those least able to obtain it.

Synonyms: ambiguity; incongruity

KAPLAN

ERUDITE

adj (ehr yuh dite) (ehr uh dite)

PARADOX

noun (<u>par</u> uh doks)

learned, scholarly, bookish

The annual meeting of philosophy professors was a gathering of the most *erudite*, well-published individuals in the field.

Synonyms: learned; scholastic; wise

impressive array

Her résumé indicates a *panoply* of skills and accomplishments.

Synonyms: array; display; range

ESCHEW

verb (ehs choo)

PANOPLY

noun (paa nuh plee)

to shun, to avoid (as something wrong or distasteful)

The filmmaker *eschewed* artificial light for her actors, resulting in a stark movie style.

Synonyms: avoid; elude; escape; evade

elaborate praise; formal hymn of praise

The director's *panegyric* for the donor who kept his charity going was heart-warming.

Synonyms: compliment; homage

ESOTERIC

adj (eh suh tehr ihk)

PANEGYRIC

noun (paan uh jeer ihk)

known or understood only by a few

Only a handful of experts are knowledgeable about the *esoteric* world of particle physics.

Synonyms: abstruse; arcane; obscure

flamboyance or dash in style and action; verve

> Leah has such *panache* when planning parties, even when they're last-minute affairs.

Synonym: flair

ESTIMABLE

adj (eh stuh muh buhl)

PANACHE

noun (puh <u>nahsh</u>)

admirable

Most people consider it *estimable* that Mother Teresa spent her life helping the poor of India.

Synonyms: admirable; commendable; creditable; honorable; laudable; meritorious; praiseworthy; respectable; venerable; worthy

lacking color or liveliness

The old drugstore's *pallid* window could not compete with Wal-Mart's extravagant display next door.

Synonyms: ashen; blanched; ghostly; pale; wan

ETHOS

noun (ēē thohs)

PALLID

adj (paa lihd)

beliefs or character of a group

It is the Boy Scouts' *ethos* that one should always be prepared.

Synonyms: culture; ethic; philosophy

to make less serious; ease

The alleged crime was so vicious that the defense lawyer could not *palliate* it for the jury.

Synonyms: alleviate; assuage; extenuate; mitigate

EULOGY

noun (yoo luh jee)

PALLIATE

verb (paa lee ayt)

speech in praise of someone

His best friend gave the *eulogy*, outlining his many achievements and talents.

Synonyms: encomium; elegy; panegyric

relating to a palace; magnificent

After living in a cramped studio apartment for years, Siobhan thought the modest one-bedroom looked downright *palatial*.

Synonyms: grand; stately

EUPHEMISM

noun (yoo fum ih zuhm)

PALATIAL

adj (puh lay shuhl)

use of an inoffensive word or phrase in place of a more distasteful one

The funeral director preferred to use the *euphemism* 'sleeping' instead of the word 'dead.'

agitated, overdone

> The lawyer's *overwrought* voice on the phone made her clients worry about the outcome of their case.

Synonyms: elaborate; excited; nervous; ornate

EUPHONY

noun (yoo fuh nee)

OVERWROUGHT

adj (oh vuhr rawt)

pleasant, harmonious sound

To their loving parents, the children's orchestra performance sounded like *euphony*, although an outside observer would have probably called it a cacophony.

Synonyms: harmony; melody; music; sweetness

excessive showiness

The *ostentation* of The Sun King's court is evident in the lavish decoration and luxuriousness of his palace at Versailles.

Synonyms: conspicuousness; flashiness; pretentiousness; showiness

EXACERBATE

verb (ihg zaas uhr bayt)

OSTENTATION

noun (ah stehn tay shuhn)

to make worse

It is unwise to take aspirin to try to relieve heartburn since instead of providing relief it will only *exacerbate* the problem.

Synonyms: aggravate; annoy; intensify; irritate; provoke

apparent

The *ostensible* reason for his visit was to borrow a book, but he secretly wanted to chat with the lovely Wanda.

Synonyms: represented; supposed; surface

EXCULPATE

verb (ehk skuhl payt) (ihk skuhl payt)

OSTENSIBLE

adj (ah <u>stehn</u> sih buhl)

to clear from blame, to prove innocent

The legal system is intended to convict those who are guilty and *exculpate* those who are innocent.

Synonyms: absolve; acquit; clear; exonerate; vindicate

to change into bone; to become hardened or set in a rigidly conventional pattern

The forensics expert ascertained the body's age based on the degree to which the facial structure had *ossified*.

EXIGENT

adj (ehk suh juhnt)

OSSIFY

verb (<u>ah</u> sih fie)

urgent; requiring immediate action

The patient was losing blood so rapidly that it was *exigent* to stop the source of the bleeding.

Synonyms: critical; imperative; needed; urgent

pompous

> Roberto soon grew tired of his date's *orotund* babble about her new job, and decided their first date would probably be their last.

Synonyms: aureate; bombastic; declamatory; euphuistic; flowery; grandiloquent; magniloquent; oratorical; overblown; sonorous

EXONERATE

verb (ihg zahn uh rayt)

OROTUND

adj (<u>or</u> uh tuhnd) (<u>ah</u> ruh tuhnd)

to clear of blame

The fugitive was *exonerated* when another criminal confessed to committing the crime.

Synonyms: absolve; acquit; clear; exculpate; vindicate

public disgrace

After the scheme to embezzle the elderly was made public, the treasurer resigned in utter *opprobrium*.

Synonyms: discredit; disgrace; dishonor; disrepute; ignominy; infamy; obloquy; shame

EXPLICIT

adj (ehk splih siht)

OPPROBRIUM

noun (uh pro bree uhm)

clearly stated or shown; forthright in expression

In Reading Comprehension, questions that ask directly about a detail in the passage are sometimes called *Explicit* Text questions.

Synonyms: candid; clear-cut; definite; definitive; express; frank; specific; straightforward; unambiguous; unequivocal

to express an opinion

At the "Let's Chat Talk Show," the audience member *opined* that the guest was in the wrong.

Synonyms: point out; voice

EXPONENT

noun (ihk spoh nuhnt) (ehk spoh nuhnt)

OPINE

verb (oh pien)

one who champions or advocates

The vice president was an enthusiastic *exponent* of computer technology.

Synonyms: representative; supporter

impossible to see through, preventing the passage of light

The heavy build-up of dirt and grime on the windows made them almost *opaque*.

Synonym: obscure

EXPURGATE

verb (ehk spuhr gayt)

OPAQUE

adj (oh <u>payk</u>)

to censor

Government propagandists *expurgated* all negative references to the dictator from the film.

Synonyms: cut; sanitize

troublesome and oppressive; burdensome

The assignment was so extensive and difficult to manage that it proved *onerous* to the team in charge of it.

Synonyms: arduous; backbreaking; burdensome; cumbersome; difficult; exacting; formidable; hard; laborious; oppressive; rigorous; taxing; trying

FALLOW

adj (faa loh)

ONEROUS

adj (<u>oh</u> neh ruhs)

dormant, unused

This field should lie *fallow* for a year so the soil does not become completely depleted.

Synonyms: idle; inactive; unseeded

too helpful, meddlesome

While planning her wedding, Maya discovered just how *officious* her future mother-in-law could be.

Synonyms: eager; intrusive; unwanted

FANATICAL

adj (fuh nah tih kuhl)

OFFICIOUS

adj (uh fihsh uhs)

acting excessively enthusiastic; filled with extreme, unquestioned devotion

The stormtroopers were *fanatical* in their devotion to the Emperor, readily sacrificing their lives for him.

Synonyms: extremist; fiery; frenzied; zealous

to stop up, prevent the passage of

> A shadow is thrown across the Earth's surface during a solar eclipse, when the light from the sun is *occluded* by the moon.

Synonyms: barricade; block; close; obstruct

FATUOUS

adj (fah choo uhs)

OCCLUDE

verb (uh <u>klood</u>)

stupid; foolishly self-satisfied

Ted's *fatuous* comments always embarrassed his keen-witted wife at parties.

Synonyms: absurd; ludicrous; preposterous; ridiculous; silly

to prevent; to make unnecessary

The river was shallow enough to wade across at many points, which *obviated* the need for a bridge.

Synonyms: forestall; preclude; prohibit

FAWN

verb (fahn)

OBVIATE

verb (ahb vee ayt)

to grovel

The understudy *fawned* over the director in hopes of being cast in the part on a permanent basis.

Synonyms: bootlick; grovel; pander; toady

stubborn, unyielding

The *obstinate* child could not be made to eat any food that he perceived to be 'yucky.'

Synonyms: intransigent; mulish; persistent; pertinacious; stubborn; tenacious

FECUND

adj (fee kuhnd) (feh kuhnd)

OBSTINATE

adj (<u>ahb</u> stih nuht)

fertile, fruitful, productive

The *fecund* couple yielded a total of 20 children.

Synonyms: flourishing; prolific

overly submissive and eager to please

> The *obsequious* new associate made sure to compliment her supervisor's tie and agree with him on every issue.

Synonyms: compliant; deferential; servile; subservient

KAPLAN

FERVID

adj (fuhr vihd)

OBSEQUIOUS

adj (uhb <u>see</u> kwee uhs)

intensely emotional, feverish

The fans of Maria Callas were particularly *fervid*, doing anything to catch a glimpse of the great opera singer.

Synonyms: burning; impassioned; passionate; vehement; zealous

indirect, evasive; misleading, devious

> Usually open and friendly, Reinaldo has been behaving in a curiously *oblique* manner lately.

Synonyms: glancing; slanted; tangential

FETID

adj (feh tihd)

OBLIQUE

adj (oh bleek)

foul-smelling, putrid

The *fetid* stench from the outhouse caused Francesca to wrinkle her nose in disgust.

Synonyms: funky; malodorous; noisome; rank; stinky

hardened in feeling, resistant to persuasion

The president was completely *obdurate* on the issue, and no amount of persuasion would change his mind.

Synonyms: inflexible; intransigent; recalcitrant; tenacious; unyielding

FLAG

verb (flaag)

OBDURATE

adj (<u>ahb</u> duhr uht)

to decline in vigor, strength, or interest

The marathon runner slowed down as his strength *flagged*.

Synonyms: dwindle; ebb; slacken; subside; wane

coin collecting

Tomas's passion for *numismatics* has resulted in an impressive collection of coins from all over the world.

FLORID

adj (flohr ihd) (flahr ihd)

NUMISMATICS

noun (nu miz maa tiks)

excessively decorated or embellished

The palace had been decorated in an excessively *florid* style; every surface had been carved and gilded.

Synonyms: Baroque; elaborate; flamboyant; ornate; ostentatious; Rococo

a subtle expression of meaning or quality

The scholars argued for hours over tiny *nuances* in the interpretation of the last line of the poem.

Synonyms: gradation; subtlety; tone

FOMENT

verb (foh mehnt)

NUANCE

noun (<u>noo</u> ahns)

to arouse or incite

The rebels tried to *foment* revolution through their attacks on the government.

Synonyms: agitate; impassion; inflame; instigate; kindle

existing in name only; negligible

A *nominal* member of the high school yearbook committee, she rarely attends meetings.

Synonyms: minimal; titular

FORD

verb (fohrd)

NOMINAL

adj (nah mihn uhl)

to cross a body of water by wading

Because of the recent torrential rains, the cowboys were unable to *ford* the swollen river.

Synonyms: traverse; wade

stinking, putrid

A dead mouse trapped in your walls produces a *noisome* odor.

Synonyms: disgusting; foul; malodorous

FORESTALL

verb (fohr stahl)

NOISOME

adj (noy suhm)

to prevent, delay; anticipate

The landlord *forestalled* T.J.'s attempt to avoid paying the rent by waiting for him outside his door.

Synonyms: avert; deter; hinder; obviate; preclude

to irritate

I don't particularly like having blue hair—I just do it to *nettle* my parents.

Synonyms: annoy; vex

FORTUITOUS

adj (fohr too ih tuhs)

NETTLE

verb (<u>neh</u> tuhl)

happening by chance, fortunate

It was *fortuitous* that he won the lotto just before he had to pay back his loans.

Synonyms: chance; fortunate; haphazard; lucky; propitious; prosperous

novice, beginner

A relative *neophyte* at bowling, Rodolfo rolled all of his balls into the gutter.

Synonyms: apprentice; greenhorn; tyro

FRACTIOUS

adj (frak shuhs)

NEOPHYTE

noun (<u>nee</u> oh fiet)

unruly, rebellious

The general had a hard time maintaining discipline among his *fractious* troops.

Synonyms: contentious; cranky; peevish; quarrelsome

new word or expression

Aunt Mable simply does not understand today's youth; she is perplexed by their clothing, music, and *neologisms*.

Synonyms: slang; slip-of-the-tongue

FRENETIC

adj (fruh neht ihk)

NEOLOGISM

noun (nee <u>ah</u> luh ji zuhm)

frantic, frenzied

The employee's *frenetic* schedule left her little time to socialize.

Synonym: corybantic; delirious; feverish; mad; rabid; wild

starting to develop, coming into existence

The advertising campaign was still in a *nascent* stage, and nothing had been finalized yet.

Synonyms: embryonic; emerging; inchoate; incipient

FRUGALITY

noun (fru gaa luh tee)

NASCENT

adj (<u>nay</u> sehnt)

tendency to be thrifty or cheap

Scroogе McDuck's *frugality* was so great that he accumulated enough wealth to fill a giant storehouse with money.

Synonyms: cheapness; economy; parsimony

lacking sophistication or experience

Inexperienced writers often are *naïve* and assume that big words make them sound smarter.

Synonyms: artless; credulous; guileless; ingenuous; simple; unaffected; unsophisticated

FURTIVE

adj (fuhr tihv)

NAÏVE

adj (nah <u>eev</u>)

secret, stealthy

Glenn was *furtive* when he peered out of the corner of his eye at the stunningly beautiful model.

Synonyms: clandestine; covert; shifty; surreptitious; underhand

lowest point

> As Joey waited in line to audition for the diaper commercial, he realized he had reached the *nadir* of his acting career.

Synonyms: bottom; depth; pit

GAMBOL

verb (gaam buhl)

NADIR

noun (nay dihr) (nay duhr)

to dance or skip around playfully

From her office, Amy enviously watched the playful puppies *gambol* around Central Park.

Synonyms: caper; cavort; frisk; frolic; rollick; romp

lacking foresight, having a narrow view or long-range perspective

Not wanting to spend a lot of money up front, the *myopic* business owner would likely suffer the consequences later.

Synonyms: short-sighted; unthinking

GARNER

verb (gahr nuhr)

MYOPIC

adj (mie <u>ahp</u> ihk) (mie <u>oh</u> pihk)

to gather and store

The director managed to *garner* financial backing from several different sources for his next project.

Synonyms: amass; acquire; glean; harvest; reap

diverse

Ken opened the hotel room window, letting in the *multifarious* noises of the great city.

Synonyms: assorted; indiscriminate; heterogenous; legion; motley; multifold; multiform; multiplex; multivarious; populous; varied

GARRULOUS

adj (gaar uh luhs) (gaar yuh luhs)

MULTIFARIOUS

adj (muhl tuh <u>faar</u> ee uhs)

tending to talk a lot

The *garrulous* parakeet distracted its owner with its continuous talking.

Synonyms: effusive; loquacious

fixed customs or manners; moral attitudes

In keeping with the *mores* of ancient Roman society, Nero held a celebration every weekend.

Synonyms: conventions; practices

GESTATION

noun (jeh stay shuhn)

MORES

noun (<u>mawr</u> ayz)

growth process from conception to birth

The longer the *gestation* period of an organism, the more developed the baby is at birth.

Synonyms: development; gravidity; pregnancy

no variation, tediously the same

The *monotony* of the sound of the dripping faucet almost drove the research assistant crazy.

Synonyms: drone; tedium

GLIB

adj (glihb)

MONOTONY

noun (muh <u>naht</u> nee)

fluent in an insincere manner; offhand, casual

The slimy politician managed to continue gaining supporters because he was a *glib* speaker.

Synonyms: easy; superficial

extremely plain or secluded, as in a monastery

> The philosopher retired to his *monastic* lodgings to contemplate life free from any worldly distraction.

Synonyms: austere; contemplative; disciplined; regimented; self-abnegating

GLOWER

verb (glow uhr)

MONASTIC

adj (muh naas tihk)

to glare; stare angrily and intensely

The cranky waiter *glowered* at the indecisive customer.

Synonyms: frown; lower; scowl

to shed hair, skin, or an outer layer periodically

The snake *molted* its skin and left it behind in a crumpled mass.

Synonyms: cast; defoliate; desquamate

GRADATION

noun (gray day shuhn)

MOLT

verb (muhlt)

process occurring by regular degrees or stages; variation in color

The paint store offers so many different *gradations* of red that it's impossible to choose among them.

Synonyms: nuance; shade; step; subtlety

to calm or make less severe

Their argument was so intense that is was difficult to believe any compromise would *mollify* them.

Synonyms: appease; assuage; conciliate; pacify

GREGARIOUS

adj (greh gayr ee uhs)

MOLLIFY

verb (<u>mahl</u> uh fie)

outgoing, sociable

She was so *gregarious* that when she found herself alone she felt quite sad.

Synonyms: affable; communicative; congenial; sociable

to soften, to lessen

A judge may *mitigate* a sentence if she decides that a person committed a crime out of need.

Synonyms: allay; alleviate; assuage; ease; lighten; moderate; mollify; palliate; temper

GRIEVOUS

adj (gree vuhs)

MITIGATE

verb (<u>miht</u> ih gayt)

causing grief or sorrow; serious and distressing

Maude and Bertha sobbed loudly throughout the *grievous* event.

Synonyms: dire; dolorous; grave; mournful

a written note or letter

Priscilla spent hours composing a romantic *missive* for Elvis.

Synonym: message

GROVEL

verb (grah vuhl)

MISSIVE

noun (<u>mihs</u> ihv)

to humble oneself in a demeaning way

Thor *groveled* to his ex-girlfriend, hoping she would take him back.

Synonyms: bootlick; cringe; fawn; kowtow; toady

a person who dislikes others

The Grinch was such a *misanthrope* that even the sight of children singing made him angry.

Synonym: curmudgeon

GUILE

noun (gie uhl)

MISANTHROPE

noun (<u>mihs</u> ahn throhp)

deceit, trickery

Since he was not fast enough to catch the roadrunner on foot, the coyote resorted to *guile* in an effort to trap his enemy.

Synonyms: artifice; chicanery; connivery; duplicity

frivolity, gaiety, laughter

Vera's hilarious jokes contributed to the general *mirth* at the dinner party.

Synonyms: glee; hilarity; jollity; merriment

GULLIBLE

adj (guh luh buhl)

MIRTH

noun (muhrth)

easily deceived

The con man pretended to be a bank officer so as to fool *gullible* bank customers into giving him their account information.

Synonyms: credulous; exploitable; naïve

to operate against, work against

Lenin *militated* against the tsar for years before he overthrew him and established the Soviet Union.

Synonyms: influence; affect; change

HAPLESS

adj (haap luhs)

MILITATE

verb (mihl ih tayt)

unfortunate, having bad luck

I wish someone would give that poor, *hapless* soul some food and shelter.

Synonyms: ill-fated; ill-starred; jinxed; luckless; unlucky

extremely careful, fastidious, painstaking

> To find all the clues at the crime scene, the *meticulous* investigators examined every inch of the area.

Synonyms: finicky; fussy; picky; precise; punctilious; scrupulous

KAPLAN

HEGEMONY

noun (hih jeh muh nee)

METICULOUS

adj (mih tihk yuh luhs)

the domination of one state or group over its allies

When Germany claimed *hegemony* over Russia, Stalin was outraged.

Synonyms: authority; power

figure of speech comparing two different things

> The *metaphor* "a sea of troubles" suggests a lot of troubles by comparing their number to the vastness of the sea.

Synonyms: allegory; analogy; simile; symbol

HERMETIC

adj (huhr meh tihk)

METAPHOR

noun (meht uh fohr) (meht uh fuhr)

tightly sealed

The *hermetic* seal of the jar proved impossible to break.

Synonyms: airtight; impervious; watertight

gaudy; falsely attractive

The casino's *meretricious* decor horrified the cultivated interior designer.

Synonyms: flashy; insincere; loud; specious; tawdry

HETEROGENEOUS

adj (heh tuh ruh jee nee uhs) (he truh jee nyuhs)

MERETRICIOUS

adj (mehr ih <u>trihsh</u> uhs)

composed of unlike parts, different, diverse

The United Nations is by nature a *heterogeneous* body.

Synonyms: assorted; miscellaneous; mixed; motley; varied

quick, shrewd, and unpredictable

Her *mercurial* personality made it difficult to guess how she would react to the bad news.

Synonyms: clever; crafty; volatile; whimsical

HOARY

adj (hohr ee) (haw ree)

MERCURIAL

adj (muhr kyoor ee uhl)

very old; whitish or gray from age

The old man's *hoary* beard contrasted starkly with the new stubble of his teenage grandson.

Synonyms: ancient; antediluvian; antique; venerable; vintage

beggar

“Please, sir, can you spare a dime?” begged the *mendicant* as the businessman walked past.

Synonyms: panhandler; pauper

HOMOGENOUS

adj (huh mah juhn uhs)

MENDICANT

noun (mehn dih kuhnt)

of a similar kind

The class was fairly *homogenous* since almost all of the students were journalism majors.

Synonyms: consistent; standardized; uniform; unvarying

dishonest

So many of her stories were *mendacious* that I decided she must be a pathological liar.

Synonyms: deceitful; false; lying; untruthful

HUSBAND

verb (huhz buhnd)

MENDACIOUS

adj (mehn day shuhs)

to manage economically; to use sparingly

The cyclist paced herself at the start of the race, knowing that if she *husbanded* her resources she'd have the strength to break out of the pack later on.

Synonym: conserve

overly sentimental

The mother's death should have been a touching scene, but the movie's treatment of it was so *maudlin* that, instead of making the audience cry, it made them cringe.

Synonyms: bathetic; mawkish; saccharine; weepy

HYPERBOLE

noun (hie puhr boh lee)

MAUDLIN

adj (mawd lihn)

purposeful exaggeration for effect

When the mayor claimed his town was one of the seven wonders of the world, outsiders classified his statement as a *hyperbole.*

Synonyms: embellishment; inflation; magnification

strict disciplinarian; one who rigidly follows rules

> A complete *martinet*, the official insisted that Pete fill out all the forms again even though he was already familiar with his case.

Synonyms: dictator; stickler; tyrant

ICONOCLAST

noun (ie kahn uh klaast)

MARTINET

noun (mahr tihn <u>eht</u>)

one who opposes established beliefs, customs, and institutions

His lack of regard for traditional beliefs soon established him as an *iconoclast.*

Synonyms: maverick; nonconformist; rebel; revolutionary

to damage, deface; spoil

Telephone poles *mar* the natural beauty of the countryside.

Synonyms: blemish; disfigure; impair; injure; scar

IDIOSYNCRACY

noun (ih dee uh sihn kruh see)

MAR

verb (mahr)

peculiarity of temperament, eccentricity

His numerous *idiosyncrasies* included a fondness for wearing bright green shoes with mauve socks.

Synonyms: humor; oddity; quirk

artificial or stilted in character

The portrait is an example of the *mannered* style that was favored in that era.

Synonyms: affected; unnatural

IGNOBLE

adj (ihg noh buhl)

having low moral standards, not noble in character; mean

The photographer was paid a princely sum for the picture of the self-proclaimed ethicist in the *ignoble* act of pick-pocketing.

Synonyms: lowly; vulgar

MANNERED

adj (maan uhrd)

capable of being shaped

Gold is the most *malleable* of precious metals; it can easily be formed into almost any shape.

Synonyms: adaptable; ductile; plastic; pliable; pliant

IMBUE

verb (ihm byoo)

MALLEABLE

adj (mah lee uh buhl) (mal yuh buhl) (mah luh buhl)

to infuse; dye, wet, moisten

Marcia struggled to *imbue* her children with decent values, a difficult task in this day and age.

Synonyms: charge; freight; impregnate; permeate; pervade

to evade responsibility by pretending to be ill

> A common way to avoid the draft was by *malingering*—pretending to be mentally or physically ill so as to avoid being taken by the Army.

Synonyms: shirk; slack

IMPASSE

noun (ihm pass) (ihm pass)

MALINGER

verb (muh ling guhr)

blocked path; dilemma with no solution

The rock slide produced an *impasse*, so no one could proceed further on the road.

Synonyms: cul-de-sac; deadlock; stalemate

a curse; a wish of evil upon another

The frog prince looked for a princess to kiss him and put an end to the witch's *malediction*.

Synonyms: anathema; imprecation

IMPECUNIOUS

adj (ihm pih kyoo nyuhs) (ihm pih kyoo nee uhs)

MALEDICTION

noun (maal ih <u>dihk</u> shun)

poor, having no money

After the stock market crashed, many former millionaires found themselves *impecunious.*

Synonyms: destitute; impoverished; indigent; needy; penniless

powerful or influential person

The entertainment *magnate* bought two cable TV stations to add to his collection of magazines and publishing houses.

Synonyms: dignitary; luminary; nabob; potentate; tycoon

IMPERTURBABLE

adj (im puhr tuhr buh buhl)

MAGNATE

noun (<u>maag</u> nayt) (<u>maag</u> niht)

not capable of being disturbed

The counselor had so much experience dealing with distraught children that she was *imperturbable*, even when faced with the wildest tantrums.

Synonyms: composed; dispassionate; impassive; serene; stoical

whirlpool; turmoil; agitated state of mind

The transportation system of the city had collapsed in the *maelstrom* of war.

Synonyms: Charybdis; eddy; turbulence

IMPERVIOUS

adj (ihm purh vee uhs)

MAELSTROM

noun (mayl struhm)

impossible to penetrate; incapable of being affected

A good raincoat will be *impervious* to moisture.

Synonyms: impregnable; resistant

plot or scheme

Tired of his enemies' endless *machinations* to remove him from the throne, the king had them executed.

Synonyms: cabal; conspiracy; design; intrigue

IMPETUOUS

adj (ihm peh choo uhs) (ihm pehch wuhs)

MACHINATION

noun (mahk uh <u>nay</u> shuhn)

quick to act without thinking

It is not good for an investment broker to be *impetuous* since much thought should be given to all the possible options.

Synonyms: impulsive; precipitate; rash; reckless; spontaneous

bright, brilliant, glowing

The park was bathed in *luminous* sunshine that warmed the bodies and the souls of the visitors.

Synonyms: incandescent; lucent; lustrous; radiant; resplendent

IMPIOUS

adj (ihm pee uhs)(ihm pie uhs)

LUMINOUS

adj (<u>loo</u> muhn uhs)

not devout in religion

The nun cut herself off from her *impious* family after she entered the convent.

Synonyms: immoral; irreverent; profane

to move slowly and awkwardly

> The bear *lumbered* towards the garbage, drooling at the prospect of the Big Mac leftovers he smelled.

Synonyms: galumph; hulk; lurch; stumble

IMPLACABLE

adj (ihm play kuh buhl) (ihm plaa kuh buhl)

LUMBER

verb (<u>luhm</u> buhr)

unable to be calmed down or made peaceful

His rage at the betrayal was so great that he remained *implacable* for weeks.

Synonyms: inexorable; intransigent; irreconcilable; relentless; remorseless; unforgiving; unrelenting

sorrowful, mournful; dismal

Irish wakes are a rousing departure from the *lugubrious* funeral services to which most people are accustomed.

Synonyms: funereal; gloomy; melancholy; somber; woeful

IMPRECATION

noun (ihm prih kay shuhn)

LUGUBRIOUS

adj (loo goo bree uhs)

a curse

Spouting violent *imprecations*, Hank searched for the person who had vandalized his truck.

Synonym: damnation

clear and easily understood

The explanations were written in a simple and *lucid* manner so that students were immediately able to apply what they had learned.

Synonyms: clear; coherent; explicit; intelligible; limpid

IMPUGN

verb (ihm pyoon)

LUCID

adj (<u>loo</u> sihd)

to call into question; to attack verbally

“How dare you *impugn* my motives?” protested the lawyer, on being accused of ambulance chasing.

Synonyms: challenge; dispute

talkative

She is naturally *loquacious*, which is a problem in situations where listening is more important than talking.

Synonyms: effusive; garrulous; verbose

INCARNADINE

adj (in car nuh deen)

LOQUACIOUS

adj (loh <u>kway</u> shuhs)

blood-red in color

At his mother's mention of his baby pictures, the shy boy's cheeks turned *incarnadine* with embarrassment.

Synonyms: reddened; ruby; ruddy

discolored from a bruise; pale; reddened with anger

André was *livid* when he discovered that someone had spilled grape juice all over his cashmere coat.

Synonyms: ashen; black-and-blue; furious; pallid

INCHOATE

adj (ihn kōh uht)

LIVID

adj (<u>lih</u> vihd)

not fully formed, disorganized

The ideas expressed in Nietzsche's mature work also appear in an *inchoate* form in his earliest writing.

Synonyms: amorphous; incoherent; incomplete; unorganized

lacking energy and enthusiasm

Listless and depressed after breaking up with his girlfriend, Raj spent his days moping on the couch.

Synonyms: fainéant; indolent; languid; lethargic; sluggish

INCULCATE

verb (ihn kuhl kayt) (ihn kuhl kayt)

LISTLESS

adj (<u>lihst</u> lihs)

to teach, impress in the mind

Most parents *inculcate* their children with their beliefs and ideas instead of allowing their children to develop their own values.

Synonyms: implant; indoctrinate; instill; preach

easily flexed, limber, agile

The *lissome* yoga instructor twisted herself into shapes that her students could only dream of.

Synonyms: graceful; lithe; supple

INDOLENT

adj (ihn duh luhnt)

LISSOME

adj (lihs uhm)

habitually lazy, idle

Her *indolent* ways got her fired from many jobs.

Synonyms: lethargic; slothful; sluggish

to treat as a celebrity

After the success of his novel, the author was *lionized* by the press.

Synonyms: feast; honor; ply; regale

INEXORABLE

adj (ihn ehk suhr uh buhl)

inflexible, unyielding

The *inexorable* force of the twister swept away their house.

Synonyms: adamant; obdurate; relentless

LIONIZE

verb (lie uhn iez)

clear, transparent

Fernando could see all the way to the bottom through the pond's *limpid* water.

Synonyms: lucid; pellucid; serene

INGENUOUS

adj (ihn jehn yoo uhs)

LIMPID

adj (<u>lim</u> pihd)

showing innocence or childlike simplicity

She was so *ingenuous* that her friends feared that her innocence and trustfulness would be exploited when she visited the big city.

Synonyms: artless; guileless; innocent; naïve; simple; unaffected

immoral; unrestrained by society

Religious citizens were outraged by the *licentious* exploits of the free-spirited artists living in town.

Synonyms: lewd; wanton

INGRATE

noun (ihn grayt)

LICENTIOUS

adj (lie <u>sehn</u> shuhs)

ungrateful person

When none of her relatives thanked her for the fruitcakes she had sent them, Audrey condemned them all as *ingrates.*

Synonyms: cad; churl

a free thinker, usually used disparagingly; one without moral restraint

The *libertine* took pleasure in gambling away his family's money.

Synonym: hedonist

INGRATIATE

verb (ihn gray shee ayt)

LIBERTINE

noun (lihb uhr teen)

to gain favor with another by deliberate effort; to seek to please somebody so as to gain an advantage

The new intern tried to *ingratiate* herself with the managers so that they might consider her for a future job.

Synonyms: curry favor; flatter

tolerant, broad-minded; generous, lavish

Cali's *liberal* parents trusted her and allowed her to manage her own affairs to a large extent.

Synonyms: bounteous; latitudinarian; munificent; permissive; progressive

INIMICAL

adj (ih nihm ih kuhl)

LIBERAL

adj (lihb uh ruhl) (lihb ruhl)

hostile, unfriendly

Even though a cease-fire had been in place for months, the two sides were still *inimical* to each other.

Synonyms: adverse; antagonistic; dissident; recalcitrant

an inappropriate lack of seriousness, overly casual

The joke added needed *levity* to the otherwise serious meeting.

Synonyms: amusement; humor

INIQUITY

noun (ih nihk wih tee)

LEVITY

noun (<u>leh</u> vih tee)

sin, evil act

“I promise to close every den of *iniquity* in this town!” thundered the conservative new mayor.

Synonyms: enormity; immorality; injustice; vice; wickedness

acting in an indifferent or slow, sluggish manner

The clerk was so *lethargic* that, even when business was slow, he always had a long line in front of him.

Synonyms: apathetic; lackadaisical; languid; listless; torpid

INNOCUOUS

adj (ih nahk yoo uhs)

LETHARGIC

adj (luh <u>thar</u> jik)

harmless

Some snakes are poisonous, but most species are *innocuous* and pose no danger to humans.

Synonyms: benign; harmless; inoffensive; insipid

trickery

> The little boy thought his *legerdemain* was working on his mother, but she in fact knew about every hidden toy and stolen cookie.

Synonyms: chicanery; conjuring

INQUEST

noun (ihn kwehst)

LEGERDEMAIN

noun (lehj uhr duh mayn)

an investigation, an inquiry

The police chief ordered an *inquest* to determine what went wrong.

Synonyms: probe; quest; research

suspicious

After being swindled once, Ruth became *leery* of strangers trying to sell things to her.

Synonyms: distrustful; guarded; wary

INSIPID

adj (in sih pid)

LEERY

adj (<u>lihr</u> ree)

lacking interest or flavor

The critic claimed that the painting was *insipid*, containing no interesting qualities at all.

Synonyms: banal; bland; dull; stale; vapid

extremely generous or extravagant

Olga gave her puppy so many *lavish* treats that it soon became overweight and spoiled.

Synonyms: extravagant; exuberant; luxuriant; opulent; prodigal; profuse; superabundant

INSURRECTION

noun (ihn suh rehk shuhn)

LAVISH

adj (laa vish)

rebellion

After the Emperor's troops crushed the *insurrection*, its leaders fled the country.

Synonyms: mutiny; revolt; revolution; uprising

to give praise, to glorify

Parades and fireworks were staged to *laud* the success of the rebels.

Synonyms: acclaim; applaud; commend; compliment; exalt; extol; hail; praise

INTER

verb (ihn tuhr)

LAUD

verb (lawd)

to bury

After giving the masses one last chance to pay their respects, the leader's body was *interred.*

Synonyms: entomb; inhume; sepulchre; tomb

potential that is not readily apparent

Latent trait testing seeks to identify skills that the test taker may have that they are not aware of.

Synonyms: concealed; dormant; inert; potential; quiescent

INTERREGNUM

noun (in tuh reg nuhm)

LATENT

adj (<u>lay</u> tnt)

interval between reigns

When John F. Kennedy was shot, there was a brief *interregnum* before Lyndon B. Johnson became president.

a state of diminished energy

The lack of energy that characterizes patients with anemia makes *lassitude* one of the primary symptoms of the disease.

Synonyms: debilitation; enervation; fatigue; languor; listlessness; tiredness; weariness

INTRACTABLE

adj (ihn traak tuh buhl)

LASSITUDE

noun (laas ih tood)

not easily managed or manipulated

Intractable for hours, the wild horse eventually allowed the rider to mount.

Synonyms: stubborn; unruly

generous giving (as of money) to others who may seem inferior

She'd always relied on her parent's *largess*, but after graduation she had to get a job.

Synonyms: benevolence; boon; compliment; favor; present

INTRANSIGENT

adj (ihn traan suh juhnt) (ihn traan zuh juhnt)

LARGESS

noun (laar <u>jehs</u>)

uncompromising, refusing to be reconciled

The professor was *intransigent* on the deadline, insisting that everyone turn in the assignment at the same time.

Synonyms: implacable; inexorable; irreconcilable; obdurate; obstinate; remorseless; rigid; unbending; unrelenting; unyielding

theft of property

The crime of stealing a wallet can be categorized as petty *larceny*.

Synonyms: burglary; robbery; stealing

INTREPID

adj (ihn treh pihd)

LARCENY

noun (laar suh nee)

fearless, resolutely courageous

Despite freezing winds, the *intrepid* hiker completed his ascent.

Synonym: brave

relating to precious stones or the art of cutting them

Most *lapidary* work today is done with the use of motorized equipment.

INUNDATE

verb (ih nuhn dayt)

LAPIDARY

adj (laa puh der ee)

to overwhelm; to cover with water

The tidal wave *inundated* Atlantis, which was lost beneath the water.

Synonyms: deluge; drown; engulf; flood; submerge

lacking energy, slow; indifferent

The *languid* cat cleaned its fur, ignoring the vicious, snarling dog chained a few feet away from it.

Synonyms: fainéant; lackadaisical; listless; sluggish; weak

INURE

verb (ih nyoor)

LANGUID

adj (laang gwihd)

to harden; accustom, become used to

Eventually, Hassad became *inured* to the sirens that went off every night and could sleep through them.

Synonyms: condition; familiarize; habituate

to ridicule with satire

> The mayor hated being *lampooned* by the press for his efforts to improve people's politeness.

Synonym: tease

INVECTIVE

noun (ihn vek tihv)

LAMPOON

verb (laam <u>poon</u>)

abusive language

A stream of *invectives* poured from Mrs. Pratt's mouth as she watched the vandals smash her ceramic frog.

Synonyms: denunciation; revilement; vituperation

to express sorrow, to grieve

The children continued to *lament* the death of the goldfish weeks after its demise.

Synonyms: bewail; deplore; grieve; mourn

INVESTITURE

noun (in ves tuh chur)

LAMENT

verb (luh mehnt)

ceremony conferring authority

At Napoleon's *investiture*, he grabbed the crown from the Pope's hands and placed it on his head himself.

Synonyms: inaugural; inauguration; induction; initiation; installation

using few words

> He was the classic *laconic* native of Maine; he talked as if he were being charged for each word.

Synonyms: concise; curt; pithy; taciturn; terse

INVIDIOUS

adj (ihn vihd ee uhs)

LACONIC

adj (luh kah nihk)

envious, obnoxious, offensive; likely to promote ill-will

It is cruel and *invidious* for parents to play favorites with their children.

Synonyms: discriminatory; insulting; jaundiced; resentful

tearful

Marcella always became *lachrymose* when it was time to bid her daughter good-bye.

Synonyms: teary; weepy

IRASCIBLE

adj (ih rah suh buhl)

LACHRYMOSE

adj (<u>laak</u> ruh mohs)

easily made angry

Attila the Hun's *irascible* and violent nature made all who dealt with him fear for their lives.

Synonyms: cantankerous; irritable; ornery; testy

fame, glory, honor

The actress happily accepted *kudos* from the press for her stunning performance in the film.

Synonyms: acclaim; accolade; encomium; homage; praise

ITINERANT

adj (ie tihn uhr uhnt)

KUDOS

noun (koo dohz)

wandering from place to place; unsettled

The *itinerant* tomcat came back to the Johansson homestead every two months.

Synonyms: nomadic; vagrant

sound of a funeral bell; omen of death or failure

When the townspeople heard the *knell* from the church belfry, they knew that their mayor had died.

Synonyms: chime; peal; toll

JARGON

noun (jahr guhn)

KNELL

noun (nehl)

nonsensical talk; specialized language

You need to master technical *jargon* in order to communicate successfully with engineers.

Synonyms: argot; cant; dialect; idiom; slang

relating to motion; characterized by movement

The *kinetic* sculpture moved back and forth, startling the museum visitors.

Synonyms: active; dynamic; mobile

JETTISON

verb (jeht ih zuhn) (jeht ih suhn)

KINETIC

adj (kih neh tihk)

to discard, to get rid of as unnecessary or encumbering

The sinking ship *jettisoned* its cargo in a desperate attempt to reduce its weight.

Synonyms: dump; eject

to set fire to or ignite; excite or inspire

With only damp wood to work with, Tilda had great difficulty trying to *kindle* the camp fire.

Synonyms: arouse; awaken; light; spark

JINGOISM

noun (jing goh ihz uhm)

KAPLAN

belligerent support of one's country

The professor's *jingoism* made it difficult for the students to participate in an open political discussion.

Synonyms: chauvinism; nationalism

KINDLE

verb (<u>kihn</u> duhl)

having a sharp edge; intellectually sharp, perceptive

With her *keen* intelligence, she figured out the puzzle in seconds flat.

Synonyms: acute; canny; quick

JOCULAR

adj (jahk yuh luhr)

KEEN

adj (keen)

playful, humorous

The *jocular* old man entertained his grandchildren for hours.

Synonyms: amusing; comical

point of time, especially where two things are joined

At this *juncture*, I think it would be a good idea for us to take a coffee break.

Synonyms: confluence; convergence; crisis; crossroads; moment

JUDICIOUS

adj (joo dih shuhs)

JUNCTURE

noun (juhnk chuhr)

sensible, showing good judgment

The wise and distinguished judge was well known for having a *judicious* temperament.

Synonyms: circumspect; prudent; sagacious; sapient

NOTES

NOTES

NOTES

NOTES